THE
SWIPE RIGHT
EFFECT

THE POWER TO GET UNSTUCK
(hint: it's not just about dating)

C.K. COLLINS

Dedication

This book is dedicated to my daughters for their unending support even on the hard days. I'm incredibly proud of you and your partners — every day, every hour, every minute. You are my joy.

And thank you to all the anonymous interviewees and special editors — you know who you are!

TABLE OF CONTENTS

TABLE OF CONTENTS

———————

BEFORE YOU READ THIS BOOK...

Before you begin reading this book, note that it includes interviews with my friends from all over the world. I decided early in the process that each person besides myself would have anonymity so that they would feel safe to share even the hardest moments of their lives.

When there are children, parents and friends involved, we all want what is best for our loved ones. Every person, every woman in this book, though, wants to help you. You are why we took the time to sit together and tell our stories. Every resource referenced is found in an appendix at the end of the book.

Because I am from Nashville, Tennessee, I thought I'd have some fun with the aliases for each of the men and women. How I chose the names came about quite naturally when I interviewed one friend. She chose Loretta and I asked, "Like Loretta Lynn?"

It hit me at that moment, I wanted to give everyone the name of a famous country music singer. All of the women have been nicknamed after a strong successful badass superstar. Some even chose their own star name. It simply works with the whole Nashville background.

In no way are any of the people associated with Dolly, Loretta, Shania, Garth, Hank or any of the other names. This is just a 'shoutout' to my hometown and the brilliance of the singers' careers.

Come to think of it – maybe I should try to interview the REAL Dolly Parton.

THE SWIPE RIGHT EFFECT

"HAVE ENOUGH COURAGE TO TRUST LOVE ONE MORE
TIME AND ALWAYS ONE MORE TIME." – MAYA ANGELOU

PREFACE

This book is for people feeling stuck.

I'm writing this for all of you who are divorced, never married, lost a partner or feel lost within your own life, your relationship or marriage and you are in search of a new way of life.

You will hear stories about my life and stories from other people who shared life lessons with me. I am eternally grateful to those who invested one of life's most precious commodities in me — TIME. This shared wisdom guided me on the path to healing and thriving. So, in gratitude, I share their stories with you.

It's important to say up front that I am no therapist, no doctor, no minister and no healer. I'm a woman who took time to meet the new me after I was divorced. I am still learning and know now that I want to always be learning, always be open to what life can show me.

Within each chapter I will tell you some of my story, how and when I accepted the wisdom shared with me and then you will hear directly from the giver of the lesson. These interviews are precious to me because I am revisiting the sad time, marveling at the beauty of the gifts and seeing with gratitude how the gift has helped shape the new me. I feel like a butterfly having come out of the cocoon.

First things first though. Let's talk about you and just how powerful you are.

You may not feel it right now but I know this to be true. Meditation, therapy, travel, prayer, support groups and exercise are just a few ways you can begin to heal. For me, it was hiking and talking issues through with friends who will be honest with me and yet not try to fix me.

You have the power to heal yourself utilizing all these methods. You choose what works for you, but the trick is — you must choose. Therefore, the real power remains within you, within your choices. The power to heal always has been within you and it still is.

The term 'swipe right' became part of our culture through a dating app where swiping someone's picture to the right meant you are choosing them. This book is about swiping right for yourself, your new life, your hopes and your dreams. I wish for you the excitement, peace and contentment that you will come to know as these parts of your life open up.

You might be in a cold dark place right now. After my divorce, I felt unwanted, lonely and used. My children were grown, my husband was gone and my business needed to be sold due to the divorce. My entire life was changing and I felt I had no choice. But then, I did choose — to take one day at a time, one step at a time.

It is funny to me that I'm about to ask this of you because I have never been great at following through with self-help books. But here goes: I'm asking anyway.

At the end of each chapter, you will find an Empowerment Practice and I'm asking you to do it. I have done all of these, in one form or another, in therapy, workshops or book studies and they have helped me. I put my own twist on them relating them to the lessons from my friends. I won't say it's fun exactly -- but I believe in the power of healing and these can help you get there.

So, there I was, feeling like a seed in the cold, dark ground – alone. It was a safe place of rest where I could gather my strength but this is not a place I wanted to stay. The miracle of joy and happiness was waiting for me.

Picture this for you. It is spring all around you and the sun is beginning to warm the earth. You, my friend, are your own sun. You make the decision to start a new life and your world begins anew. Yes, other people will come into your life and shine light. But it is your own divine light that will heal from within I know this from experience.

THIS BOOK IS LIKE THE MOON IN THAT IT IS SIMPLY AND MAGICALLY REFLECTING THE LIGHT AND LOVE OF OTHERS SO THAT IT CAN BE SHARED WITH YOU.

While you are working through your past, your present and moving toward your exciting future, I want to suggest you use a visualization and meditation technique I introduce in the preface empowerment practice. Use this visualization when times are hard and when they are good. Use it when you are sad and happy. Close your eyes, breathe and just do it. It might not feel right at first, but then something inside will change.

My hope for each of you is that you find the lessons to be helpful in your own life. Some lessons didn't resonate from the beginning. Sometimes it was a year later before it hit me (like a lightning bolt).

So as you read, tuck away what resonates and keep it in your heart. The only promise I can make you is that if you open your heart to healing, it can and will happen. Remember lesson number one -- you already have the power that can heal you.

Preface Empowerment Practice: See Yourself Growing

Visualization is a practice which requires repetition. If it works for Olympic athletes, it can work for you. It's a small, practical thing that will provide a safe place for your heart and mind.

I have provided a recording for you, but you can also record this for yourself on your smart phone and listen to it in the car, on your walks, in bed before you go to sleep.

My favorite flower is the daisy and that's my end result in this visualization. You have the freedom and power to choose what you want to be. It is just for you, so let's begin.

Take five deep breaths. Count to five as you breath in, hold for three seconds, and count to five as you breath out. Clear your mind and picture the breath coming in and out of your lungs.

When you reach a state of relaxation, begin the recording.

MEDITATION:

The time has come. Your seed is ready to transform into a beautiful, glorious flower.

Winter is over and the day grows longer. More sun comes each day to warm the earth.

The miracle of life and rebirth stand ready.

As the light of the sun warms the earth, your shell begins to slowly crack open. A small fragile stem peaks out, searching for the light.

Each day, the stem will grow and become stronger and stronger. The tender green shoot reaches for the warm earth, the life-giving light.

Then a miracle happens – the plant forms life-giving roots which grow deeper and stronger.

Days go by and a complex, fragile bud begins to form. It opens ever so slowly.

The petals release one at a time like tiny little fingers and reach for the light. The flower absorbs the light -- reaching higher and higher each moment of the day.

The flower rests deeply and soundly at night. While the flower rests, the stems, the petals, the roots and the very core of the flower utilize the power of the light to grow and flourish.

The beauty and resources of the flower begin to bring joy and life to other beings- bees, birds, humans.

Within the flower, new life begins to form. New seeds are formed within this beautiful flower.

These seeds will bring life-sustaining joy and happiness to the world as you release them.

The process is eternal, the pattern of growth and giving and rebirth.

You have it within you to continue to grow. You are a bringer of light, joy and happiness.

Reach, reach, reach.

FAITH IS TAKING THE FIRST STEP EVEN WHEN YOU DON'T SEE THE WHOLE STAIRCASE. — MARTIN LUTHER KING, JR.

———————

CHAPTER 1:
FIRST STEPS

For every heart, the first steps will be different. Every person has to deal with their loss, betrayal and pain on their own time.

There is a long list of ways to take the first step, including therapy, faith groups, divorce classes, grief support groups, travel, self-improvement books and the list goes on. I pretty much used everything at my disposal.

For good or for bad, I was so anxious to move on. My marriage had been on the rocks for six years, and once the reason for the disconnection revealed itself, I had to go and go NOW.

In 2011, I knew deep to my core something was wrong, and I was fighting for my 24-year marriage. I tried to transform myself into whatever it was I thought it was that my husband wanted. I began running. I lost weight. I went to the football games. I tried to spend less time on my company. I stopped going to church. I tried to plan date nights. All for naught.

My marriage ended dramatically in 2017. There was trauma that came from that experience of betrayal and grief for me – and for my children. I was shaken to my core and my hands were literally shaking all the time. I was exhibiting a physical reaction to the mental pain, the trauma.

After the split appeared to be final, our marriage counselor recommended that I see another therapist for PTSD, post traumatic stress disorder. I thought he was crazy until I started looking at my daily life and how different I was as a person. I had lost myself, I felt stuck, and I feared I would never be that confident, happy and vivacious woman again.

On top of the trauma of the split, the memory of a long-buried sexual assault from high school was resurfacing. I had kept it to myself since I was 15, hidden it from everyone; and although I thought I had taken care of it, there were unresolved issues. Now with the new trauma, flashbacks of the assault were happening. The marriage counselor did me the biggest favor of all by sending me to the new PTSD therapist when he did.

Adding to all this, I had a self-imposed deadline — pressure! I was leaving for the Camino de Santiago pilgrimage, by myself, at the end of April 2018. This is a 500-mile hike through southern France and northern Spain. It's a spiritual journey that has been trekked for more than 1,000 years. The people who walk it are called pilgrims. I was already a distance runner and had faith that training would physically prepare me for the journey. The mental challenge was going to be the hard part.

This was a dramatic step I was taking, traveling to another country, hiking alone for 500 miles and facing all the demons divorce presents....alone.

The night before I left, my daughters and I gathered at our home. We all piled into my big bed with our beloved golden retriever and held on to each other. They believed in me and they told me so. They were proud of me and I knew that their faith in me was going to get me through the tough moments and hours on the trail. It was a great sendoff.

Taking the Camino journey ended up being the best thing I ever did for myself. My literal first steps to get unstuck.

Start Letting Go of the Pain

In my non-clinical opinion, it is impossible to move on without settling in with the pain, allowing yourself to feel the pain and then letting go of the pain of the past.

I took a course offered by bestselling author Katherine Woodward Thomas. The book and the course are titled, *Calling in "The One."* Thomas's book, which is also available in an online video workshop on Mindvalley, walks you through envisioning your future, your partner and your fulfilled desire for true love. But then, she gets right to the heart of the matter. She leads you down a path where you work on yourself. That course was one of many, many things I have done to gain peace in my life and I highly recommend both the book and the workshop.

Many of us have pain from the past that we don't even realize is affecting our choices in life. Pain from abusive parents, bullying, abandonment, neglect and much more, can surface when we are working through our past.

Thomas does a remarkable job helping you identify your pain, find your patterns and name them for what they are. Most importantly, you must find a way to recognize and take responsibility for what has happened in the past. Because now you are going forward and you are going to stop making those mistakes, stop repeating negative behaviors and you are going to find a new life.

In this chapter, you will meet my friend Brandi from Sweden. We met on the Camino de Santiago hike in May 2018. In fact, she was the very first person I met on the journey.

We met the night we arrived in Bayonne, France, which is one of the many possible locations to start the Camino from. We ended up having dinner and sharing our stories as to why we were there. We were immediately vulnerable with each other — a willingness to show our emotion and allow our weaknesses to be seen or known. This was very impactful on my Camino experience.

We walked to the bus together in the morning, rode the bus up to St. Jean Pied de Port and we walked to the pilgrim office to get our Pilgrim Passport. These are the credentials that would allow us to stay at the albergues[1], or pilgrim hostels.

I didn't think I would ever see her again. We hugged and I watched her walk away. I was so grateful to have met someone and connected so quickly. Little did I know I would see her the next evening in a pilgrim mass. We walked together the next day and she said two things that changed my life.

---

[1] Albergue is a hostel that is for pilgrims hiking the camino. You must have pilgrim credentials to stay at the facility.

BELOW IS THE FIRST OF THE STORIES OF LESSONS TAUGHT BY MY FRIENDS AND I WILL REVEAL THE SECOND OF BRANDI'S STORIES IN CHAPTER 10!

What Do You Want For Yourself?

"What are you hoping for in your new life?" Brandi asked me.

You know those moments where you just go blank? Well that was me. I knew what I *didn't* want more than I knew what I did.

She asked if I had ever made a vision board. I had not, but I'd seen them and heard of them. I had never tried it before.

She shared with me how she had started making vision boards several years back. She included her personal goals, work goals and family goals and she shared examples. The process was placing photos, text and clippings on a board/poster that would spark the vision for that year.

But here I was on a trail with a 20 pound backpack and no cork board.

"Well, I guess I'll do that when I get home," I said.

"Take out your phone and open your notes app," she says. "Let's talk for a few minutes about what you DO want in your life. What makes you happy? Write down a few words about your future," she said.

So, I started a list of what makes me happy:

DANCING
TRAVELING
RUNNING IN A NEW CITY
MEETING PEOPLE
PHYSICAL EXERTION
EXERCISE CHALLENGES
KISS BEHIND MY EAR
HUGS FROM BEHIND
LONG, SLOW DINNER WITH FRIENDS
HOLDING HANDS
MORNING SEX
LONG SLOW KISSES
KISSES DOWN MY SPINE
SHARING BOOKS

Then goals started to emerge:

TRAVELING WITH MY DAUGHTERS
DATING A DOG LOVER
HIKING WITH MY PARTNER
AMOUNT OF $ WHEN I SELL MY BUSINESS
FINANCIAL SECURITY POST-SALE
SECURE IN LOVE WITH NO DOUBTS
EMPLOYMENT THAT BRINGS TRAVEL AND GROWTH
LIVE BY THE OCEAN

Over the duration of the seven-week Camino, this list became a place I could turn to and remind myself what made me feel good. I discussed the list with others and added to it along the way.

I had felt physically alone for a long time and when I started writing down these physical pleasures that I envisioned for myself, it became easier to feel it again. I hardly remembered how much I loved these things and how much of a physical creature I am. The seed was re-planted for me.

As I wrote further about how much money I wanted if I were to sell my business, I began to see my life without the day-to-day of the business. I was able to see past the sadness of giving up something I built. And it turned out, I DID get what I wrote down and I believe that early statement of what it was worth made a difference in how I approached the sale.

DID I MANIFEST IT? DID PRAYING WORK? I BELIEVE SO.

I am purposefully simplifying this process just so you have an example. It doesn't have to be intimidating or difficult. You don't have to take photos or cut pictures out of a magazine. You can just start with a list of words.

When I was around four years into the process of healing, I wanted some accountability for my new life on sabbatical. I began working with a life coach and she asked me to create a new vision board for myself. However, she had a new twist.

"Since you are a writer, why don't you write your own future story," she said. "Write about your new life and how it feels to be there. Put some time parameters on the vision and be as specific as you can."

I absolutely dreaded the exercise, but I was so glad she gave me a deadline! For some reason, I was afraid to write down my dreams – even though it had worked for me before. I share this so you know that I understand it is hard for most people. So if it is hard for you, you are not alone.

Once I got started though, I couldn't stop. I could have been writing a freaking romance novel! This showed me where my heart was focusing.

I loved how my life looked in the future. I was inspired by the kindness, gratitude and love I could see in my future. My heart, like the Grinch, grew 10 times in size that day. I felt the positivity of the vision surrounding me, holding me gently and the wind in my face as I sailed into that future.

Brandi Interview

I'd like for you to meet Brandi for yourself, my friend from the Camino. In each chapter, you will meet a person who has made a difference in my life. Sometimes it is a simple lesson and sometimes it is a deep, searing, painful lesson. But all these lessons have taken me this far and I want you to have the gift of what was so generously shared with me.

Kelly

It's been five years since we hiked together in Spain. Can you give me your background and what you're doing now?

Brandi

In 2015, I had a stroke. And that was not easy because my youngest son was only two months old. So, it was hard. But what I came to realize was that I knew everything was going to be fine. I didn't know how, but I just knew.

I also knew that I had made myself sick. I didn't know how, if it was something that I did or did not do, but I knew. And I knew that I had a part in it.

After I recovered from the stroke, I went back to school, because I wanted to help other people. While in school, I realized I need to help myself. I went to school for three years to become a specialist that works with energy and hypnosis.

So the first year in school, I learned about myself, intellectually and mentally, how my upbringing still affected me, what I had been through, why and everything that happened. And then the second year, I took classes to become a 12-step program therapist.

I was able to see what I had done, because it's so easy when you get sick. And I mean, it's always someone else's fault because of this or that. But the 12-step program was really good for me, because I got to see my responsibility with everything.

Kelly
How did the hypnosis play into your growth and healing?

Brandi
One of my sessions in hypnosis, I got to see my childhood trauma.

My mom was a single mother. When she was 24 years old and I was six she had her first seizure in epilepsy. I can still remember the apartment and everything in it. She had this grand mal seizure where she fell to the floor.

I remember her doing that and I'm trying to wake her up. Then I don't have any memory at all after that. My mom has told me that I ran outside calling at the neighbor's doors, screaming, 'my mother is dying,' or something like that.

Because I have always been able to talk about that happening without any emotions coming through, I thought I had worked through it. I mean, I didn't even think it affected me.

Kelly
Right. I know exactly what you mean.

Brandi
And then during the hypnosis, I got to see what was happening. I can also understand the unconscious decision I made at the time when the trauma was happening. I told myself that I have to take care of my mother. And that's a decision that has lived with me. I

have been taking care of my mother, I have been taking care of my boyfriends and my job.

And I have been so good and nice to everyone. But myself.

The other decision was that -- this is really scary -- all those emotions. I don't want to feel anything. My biggest issue is that I haven't let myself feel. Because in my family, we didn't talk about feelings and emotions, right?

You just...pretend it doesn't exist. So of course, when you think about it, where do our feelings and emotions go if we don't allow ourselves to feel them?

It stays in the body. Now I know why I have had so many physical problems.

The third year of schooling was the energy and hypnosis therapies because I wanted to work with people with emotional stress.

I started my therapy practice in 2017 before the Camino. I had to challenge myself because I'm introverted and starting my business and being new to things was uncomfortable to me. I want to know everything without having to do anything.

Kelly
"I want to be perfect." That's what I'm hearing.

Brandi
Yeah. I have been working with the therapist job till May or June this year. Throughout the COVID [pandemic], I tried to do this work online, which worked perfectly fine. You can do it over

Zoom[2]. So that was something really interesting, because I can work with clients all over the world if I want to.

Kelly

I didn't think that would work with hypnosis. That's so interesting.

Brandi

I have tried pretty much everything to work through things about my health problems – blaming it on other people, going to the doctor, getting medicine, just doing everything except doing the work. Taking control of my health is why I'm back at my old job, which is a law firm, working as an assistant with the administration, because it's well paid.

I have three boys, they are soon to be 8, 10 and then 14. So I have promised myself that during this September to New Year, I'm going to just have one job. I have been, for almost a year, working at the law firm, and my own business and having three boys.

Right now, it feels nice to be able to earn some money and just be taking care of myself. I know my time is coming for what I'm supposed to do and this is just the time to take care of myself because it's easy to burn yourself out.

I'm 49. So next year when I'm walking (the Camino) again, I'm turning 50 during the summer. That's my birthday present for myself!

---

[2] Zoom is a video conferencing platform.

It's interesting to see the shifts. When I worked as a therapist, it was like, "This is my mission. This is what I'm going to do, I will never retire from this. This is my calling."

And it still is. But right now, I feel like the world needs to come together so I can come back and do what I'm supposed to do. I can't explain it. But I'm just taking care of myself for a while.

Kelly
I'm going to dive in and ask some more questions. Thank you for the background. That was perfect. Your partner now is your second partner, right?

Brandi
My oldest son is now 14. I had him with a separate partner and then 12-13 years ago, I met my partner, who I live with now, and we have two boys.

Kelly
OK, so total of three boys. When you had that big change in your life, you had your son and you were starting over, was there a specific thing that you look back on now that helped you move forward?

Brandi
From what I understand now, I grew up in a dysfunctional family. So I didn't get the tools I needed. And because of that, when I met someone, and had a relationship with someone, it was always dysfunctional.

With my first partner, we had a good relationship, but at the end, I knew it wasn't going to last. I was changing. That was the thing. I was changing. And I was scared to finish it. Because that was what I knew.

I also don't like conflicts. But I would say the strength came because I knew I had to do this for my son. That was my source of strength, because I wanted him to grow up with a strong mother. I don't think I would have prioritized myself. I was too scared, but he gave me the strength.

Kelly
A theme I'm seeing is when the woman started changing, she couldn't stay.

Brandi
When I left, it was so easy. I mean, we ended our relationship on good terms. We were both fine doing this. But I would say, later on, we started having a bit of trouble when our son was going to be with me and with him, and, you know, we started arguing about nonsense, really.

At that point, it was so easy for me to say, you know, it's his fault. He's a bad person, he is this and that. And he did that. I was almost like a saint. And I remember something he told me once, when we were living together.

He said, "You know what, it's not so easy. It's not easy to live with someone who is so perfect."

And he was swearing. He was really angry. And I was like what are you doing? When I started my reflection, when I went back to school, I got to see what he meant.

I know I wasn't easy to stay with because I wanted and needed to have control over things. So because of my need, I could be really manipulative. And I wouldn't let him in, I would do everything.

And then I would go back to him and say, "Oh, my Lord, I have to do everything. You don't help me."

I'm really grateful for our experience, because both of us have learned and we have a good relationship. I still love him as a person because he gave me our son, but we can't live together. It's not that kind of love. But I can totally see why he came into my life.

So therefore, I'm really grateful. It wasn't fun then. But today, you can see it from a different angle, you know.

Kelly
That's really helpful. I think that's also becoming a theme, the need to have control or need to be perfect, which I wasn't expecting at all. And so I love that you shared that.

When you went out on your own, were there any interesting lessons? All of a sudden you're a single mom and you're starting over.

Brandi
We ended our relationship and we separated in November 2009. And in late March 2010, I met my partner now. I wasn't planning on it. I was really tired of men. I had no interest at all in men.

We were out at a club and I started talking to him and we live on the same island in Stockholm, which is unusual. And everything was so easy and he has had so much patience with me.

I didn't want him to meet my son for like, six months. I had to do everything my way because otherwise I would probably have said this isn't for me.

He is actually the one person that has helped me find peace inside of me to get out of the stress. You know when you have someone that creates a space for you where you feel safe? He has done that for me.

If I wanted to go walk the Camino, he would say take the time you need. Now I want to quit my job and work as a therapist, he says go ahead, being supportive.

I'm so blessed to have met this man. He's the most wonderful man ever, just making me safe. Being safe is something that I didn't have when I grew up.

To do all this self-reflection takes a lot of energy. You can't do it if you're in a bad relationship because then you're in fight or flight mode all the time. Either you stay in it and fight, or you flee.

Kelly
Interesting. It's like the Camino, I noticed that people kept making space for me to talk something through or I made space for them to share. And I always got so much out of it, learning from their experiences and just seeing how open their heart was.

On the Camino, it's so reciprocal. If you make space for somebody, you will also get something out of it. The Camino pilgrims are so open and you just get right to the heart of the matter.

"Hi, I'm Kelly. My husband cheated on me and I'm here starting over." That's my elevator speech. It got to be that short.

Brandi
That's a good thing, though.

Kelly
I've shared my memory of us talking about the vision boards with my readers.

I think it's important that a lot of what I wrote down on my vision board happened. It even happened in my timeline which was a really good lesson to me. Law of attraction!

It was a good lesson for me to be specific, don't just write what you want – say, I want it by my birthday in December, or I want to sell my business by October. I want to sell it before my divorce.

I want to talk with you about how you started doing vision boards, and when you started, what were you hoping to accomplish?

Brandi

I think that the first time I started doing vision boards, I was in my 30s. It wasn't like I did it every year but it was something that I was aware of almost every New Year's Eve. Next year, I want to exercise more or whatever. I would say that my stroke woke me up.

Even though I had made vision boards, it's easy to wish for things but not to do the work or not to believe in it.

I would say, the first years, I played it safe because I didn't want to get it wrong. I didn't ask for 'that' because I didn't believe that it would happen.

I would say after my stroke, it has become more clear. What I learned with the Camino is that I can get whatever I want but I need to use my subconscious mind. On this conscious level, I can write down 'I want to be a millionaire and I want this big house and I want to go there.'

Well, what if I had this little voice in my head saying 'No, you can't have it. No, you're not worthy of it. No, you're never gonna have it.'

Kelly

'I'm not worthy' is such a thing.

Brandi

I still use vision boards and I have screenshots on my phone. So every time I pick it up, I have something I like to see in the picture. It can be my boys as a reminder that I want to be a good mom, I want to have happy kids and I want to be available for them. And that's why I chose to do what I do right now. Because they are at an age where they need me.

Kelly

This is such an important age.

Brandi

I still do vision boards and more and more in my head, I would say, because I'm trusting whatever signs I didn't get before. Now I get signs more often. I try to do whatever I'm drawn to do.

It's also important because – where your energy goes, that's what you will get. So it's an important thing to just think about, what do I want? Because I don't know about you, but time flies. It's like, holy crap!

Kelly

Recently, I was watching a video by Brené Brown, an influential researcher who has studied shame and vulnerability. In the Ted-talk style presentation, called *The Call to Courage,* that she did for Netflix, she says time is our most fleeting and precious commodity. And you just can't get it back. That really stuck with me.

My next question is what would you share with others who are starting over and wanting to do a vision board? I like what you were saying about the subconscious, like make sure that you're aligning your subconscious.

Brandi

That's an important thing. I mean, when you do a vision board, you can do it in whatever way you want to. I had a big piece of paper, and I cut pictures or sayings from magazines and I put it on the board.

Some years, I just wrote down what I wanted. Just be specific. Not like, I want a man, you know? No, you need to dig deeper. What do I need? What do I want?

Kelly

And to 'mirror that' is my new thing. Yeah, ask yourself, are you willing to mirror those traits or that lifestyle? If I want empathy, then I need to have empathy.

Brandi

I think we are energy beings so we are drawn to whatever kind of energy we are. Now I know, I understand that every person that I meet, I mirror myself in that person. So if I look at you, and I feel like you are angry, I stop and think, 'Oh, it has nothing to do with you. It's actually about how I'm feeling, not them.'

Kelly

Yes, thank you.

I also have questions that have evolved as I've been talking to people, because I think it'd be interesting to see what everybody says, so I have four common questions I am asking everyone.

At this point in your life, what feeds your soul?

Brandi

I would say that when I die, I will not remember the money that I have had. I would see that connection with other people, my family, the close bonds that I've created, is what I can take with me on the other side.

And life hasn't always felt like it, but life is a true blessing. And when you stop trying to say that it's their fault that this happened, or I feel like this is because of that and just take a step back.

I really like Tony Robbins saying that "Life doesn't happen to you. It's happened for you."

You know, when I look back? I wouldn't change a thing. I wouldn't. I mean, it hasn't been pleasant, no, but I wouldn't change anything.

And that is such a gift, to be able to say that. Life has been really hard sometimes and it has been a journey. It still is and it's amazing. I mean, I hope I get to live to 100, especially if I'm healthy.

Kelly
OK, thank you for that.

I just took part in a workshop called *Calling in "The One"* and was introduced to the idea of self-soothing. In my whole life, I'd never heard that term.

The teacher says healthy people know how to, when they get upset, calm themselves down. They know what they need to do for themselves whether it's take a shower or take a hot bath.

So when you have those moments, what do you do for yourself to self soothe?

Brandi
I would say that, first of all, I need to breathe. Because if I don't deeply breathe, it will make everything 10 times worse.

Sometimes I need to change my thoughts. When you have a scary thought in your head, you need to change that. Because it's hard to feel wonderful when you have negative thoughts.

You can try to count backwards or whatever works for you.

What I didn't do before, which I have become so much better at, is if I need to talk to someone, I will call someone who can help me. I'm not alone.

And that's one thing that I know, when I'm working as a therapist, pretty much everyone that finds me and that I'm working with, they have similar experiences in life, their upbringing. So I would call someone who I know can help me.

And it's not the easy way. Because the people that I talk to, they are really sharp, really good therapists, they will push your buttons.

But I know that I need to face whatever I'm feeling. So for me, especially since I have a history of pushing down everything, I tried to do the opposite. Because I know what happens if I don't -- I get physically sick.

Kelly
What are you hopeful for?

Brandi
I am hopeful. In general, I would say, if you look at the world right now, it's easy to get caught up in what's happening in the outer world. I can't change that.

If I can change something or if I want to make a difference, I can do that too. And then I won't be "sweet" and you know, "oh, peace and love." If it's something that is worth fighting for, I will do that. But if I can't, or if I don't want to, I just feel it's better to be the energy that I want the world to be.

Kelly

It's almost like you're hopeful to be hopeful.

Brandi

Yeah. That's what I mean. I want to be hopeful. I don't want to be doomsday.

Kelly

That's so interesting to hear you say that.

OK. Any last advice for people going through a big change?

Brandi

Trust! If you want a change in your life, turn to someone who has done the work that you want to do. Because you will get to the finish line much faster.

Kelly

That's great advice.

Brandi

I think that, especially when I was working as a therapist, the people who found me have the similar experience that I have. I have a lot of knowledge, insights about what worked for me and what didn't work for me. I can tell you about them so you don't have to make the same mistakes.

Kelly

Oh, I love that – you get to the finish line faster. I think that's very true, very wise.

That's why I want to write this book. I feel like everybody's not going to be able to get to meet Julia in Argentina and Brandi from Sweden and beyond. I've just been so blessed and part of it is because I had the guts to get out and go do it. I could have sat at home and freaked out.

I did go to therapy, but not just therapy. I knew I had to make big changes.

It never occurred to me I would meet all the wonderful people I've met and learn all the wonderful things I've learned. I just happened to go. I listened to myself, my intuition. That's probably my personal lesson; you've got to listen to yourself.

Brandi
And I mean, when it comes down to it, we are all responsible for our lives. It's my responsibility to make myself happy. I can't put that on anyone else. So I like the saying, "You are the painter of your own life." You create your own life. Everything that I have decided, unconsciously or consciously, has made me who I am today.

I'm also grateful. It's so much fun to see you again. I can't imagine it's been almost five years. In a way, it feels like a long time and now I could sit and talk to you for 10 hours. I think that's the soul bond that we share. And that's so much greater.

Empowerment Practice 1: Create Your Vision Board

Creating a vision board is not a cut-and-dry system. You have to follow where your heart leads. What is the lowest "barrier to entry" for you?

Is your heart leading you to primarily use words, similar to my initial notes app brain dump? Use outline form if that is what feels good.

Are you a visual person and pictures most appeal to you? Use a poster board collage with images that inspire you or choose a digital vision board application.

Choose your method of vision board and give yourself a deadline for a completed first draft. This deadline should be just a few days because you have other projects ahead. This does not have to be perfect. This is the beginning of a process!

Focus your board on multiple aspects of your life, such as healthy habits, relationships, travel, finances and career.

When you feel you have a good first draft, share it with someone you trust. Don't "sell" them on your vision board. Ask them what they see and listen. Just listen.

Sit with the project and the feedback for two days and then revisit the project. Likely, you will have some revisions or additions as you have thought about it throughout the week.

Make it a practice to revisit the vision board monthly and assess what's happening. I believe you will be delighted how your vision comes to life.

CHAPTER 2:
YOU ARE ENOUGH

When you have spent your entire life doing what you truly believed was right, it CAN feel satisfying and rewarding. However, when you find out that very same life is falling apart, it WILL feel devastating and frightening.

All of a sudden, you feel like your life, your beliefs, your contributions were not enough.

I've had many discussions with friends who lived the same middleclass life. Graduate high school. Graduate college. Get a job. Get married. Have kids. Get those kids through school and send them on their way to do the same thing.

This was what I believed I was meant to do and who I was meant to be. I thought I had done my best.

For some people, the marriage was never to be. For others, kids were never to come. And some people studied hard for a career that turned out to be empty and unfulfilling.

We all find our way through life with varying degrees of ease or difficulty. But what you don't see on Facebook or Instagram is that we ALL have problems. Yes, all of us.

When my marriage with Garth [my soon to be ex] hit the fan, I felt ashamed, desperate and alone. I had been suffering for years, feeling unloved in my marriage. I shared with good friends on a peripheral level that my marriage had changed, but I didn't understand why.

> But being a "winner," a "perfect wife," and "determined," I thought all I had to do was change and be better.

It would all be OK. Surely, if I did that, it would be enough.

When I began to let others into the big scary secret — that my life isn't perfect — it was a relief. A weight was lifted from my shoulders but it was no less frightening. My deep desire to be happy, wanted and unconditionally loved was still there. I still wanted that dream life I had envisioned lasting to old age. How about you? "I still want _____." You fill in the blank.

The Good Times

I was married for 30 years. For 24 of them, we were a team, we were doing life and we were happy. I believe that.

We loved spending time together whether it was boating, cooking, entertaining, playing Santa Claus, sporting events, family vacations or hanging with the kids. We really loved and laughed our way through life.

I fell in love with Garth the summer after my freshman year in college at the age of 19. He played softball with my father on a men's team and he quickly fit seamlessly into my family. My dad later bragged that he had picked Garth for me.

I remember watching him with kids at the pool and how sweet he was with them, and telling my mom that I believed he was destined to be a good father. And he was and is a good father. His parents and mine were all great role models.

One of the reasons I believe we stayed a tight unit was because we moved eight times in 11 years for his job. We were out there in the world raising our kids without the daily support of our families. We had to be there for each other or it wouldn't have worked.

We loved being parents to our children and being involved in their activities. He was the soccer coach and I was the room mom. We had a great life.

I want to honor and recognize the good years we had. I appreciate what we had and who we were. My mom recently said to me, "I never thought this would have happened to you. You were both so in love and you had so much fun."

I heard this a lot after our split. I remember we had even been referred to as the "homecoming couple" because we just fit together.

And then things changed.

Breaking My Silence

My faith in my husband and in myself was shaken and I was afraid. He just didn't look at me the same way anymore. There it was, my biggest fear, being alone. I would be with my husband in the same room of our home and I would feel so incredibly alone.

When I finally admitted to myself that my marriage was over, the first person I called was my friend Crystal. For eight years, we had been in a "small group" at church that gathered for theological discussion as well as support and accountability. Because of our long friendship, and because I knew her story of infidelity and divorce (you will read about this in Chapter 6), I hoped she would know what to do.

The second person was my sister-in-law, Carrie. I needed Carrie's immediate support to gather the strength to talk to her husband and my brother who is also my financial advisor. I needed to understand, as soon as possible, how our finances were going to be affected by the divorce. On top of that, telling people so close to both of us was going to be a huge step for me because I knew it was something I wouldn't be able to take back. Carrie was aghast, sorrowful and supportive. She did all she could do — listen.

Carrie helped set a time where I could speak to my brother in private the next day so I didn't have to go to his office.

After telling Carrie that morning, I headed home to get cleaned up. The challenge of getting ready for work every day was exhausting. I loved my work, but I didn't want to go through the motions. I wanted to crawl in bed and cry — which, of course, was the worst thing for me.

I made it to the office and tried to focus on the company. Shortly after, Carrie walked in. She shut my office door and sat down with me. She handed me a gift and asked me to open it.

The gift was two bracelets.

One said "I am enough" and the second said "My story is not over."

I was so touched and immediately put them on. These bracelets reminded me every day, all day, that I was loved. And many people stopped me after seeing the bracelet "I am enough" and shared that it touched them to see those words. Some even told me their own story.

Carrie began to tell me a story about her friend Faith and how those three powerful words had helped her take tough steps toward a new life. I'm going to let Faith tell you her story because she does it best.

Faith Interview

In September 2022, I interviewed Faith about her experience. This is our conversation. The last four questions are common to every interview. I include them because I believe their perspective will help you as they have helped me.

Kelly

I've shared with the readers how Carrie came to my office and brought the bracelets and shared your story. And so, I would love for you to tell me how you got to that place because I think about that bracelet on my arm — people commented on it all the time. And those three words are very powerful.

Faith

I am enough. They are very powerful. And you'll have to excuse me if I get emotional. You mentioned something earlier, the place from where you're writing this book, and I think that is going to be probably the overall theme in my life — gratitude.

I come from perfectionism. I'm very much a perfectionist. I grew up in a family that expected it. I expected it of myself, I expected of others. So perfectionism is very much part of my life. It is what motivates me. But it also is what debilitates me at times.

So if I see an opportunity to do something that I want to do, I'm going to try to do it to the best of my ability. And marriage was one of those things. Family is one of those things. I expect a lot of myself and I expect a lot of my partner as well.

And I think those expectations throughout time build upon one another and that could be a good thing, but it could also be a bad thing. I think through the latter part of my marriage, when we were raising children and I was trying to be the perfect mom, I was trying to be the perfect wife.

But at the time, the kids needed me so much more than he did. Even though he had those expectations of me and I wanted to fulfill them, they weren't my priority. I struggled a lot with that through the latter part of my marriage because I knew I was failing him in those ways. But it wasn't important enough to me to do those things.

And then after the divorce, those things became even more prominent. But I look at my life, and I look at my children, and I look at our other family members and I feel like I chose the right thing. I'm just so thankful that even though we went through those trials, the outcome was still good.

I had to accept that I didn't have this nuclear, together family that I thought I would always have. A lot of the time we were separated. I mean, he was gone for work. And my kids, Liam chose to go to school out of state, Chris stayed in our hometown, Elizabeth was just here.

And so we were kind of fragmented everywhere. I probably felt like I failed them so much even though I was trying so hard to be perfect.

To look back and to see that it all turned out OK even through my failures. I got to the point where I accepted that I'm not perfect. And that life is not perfect. I'm OK with the decisions that I make.

I want to live life without regrets. I'm always going to make mistakes, but if I learn from those mistakes, then I can't really regret those mistakes. So that is the thing. I'm going to try my best to do my best. But if I fail, it's OK.

I have a hard time failing though. I really do. I will look at that one failure so much more than I look at all the good that I've done. I think just going back and seeing the results of my decisions, good or bad. It all washed out in the end and everyone is seemingly OK but I am gonna be honest, I still struggle from time to time.

I don't struggle so much with my divorce because I can truly look at that relationship and know that we are better off apart. I know that I'm actually in a better place than I would have been had I stayed. I can see that. Does that make sense?

I still struggle at times with not being fully enough. I think voices from my childhood very much fuel that. I don't know that it has so much to do with my marriage as it does just from a childhood — you can do more and you can do better.

Kelly

I'm writing about that too — dealing with your past.

Faith

So that you don't repeat that? Yes.

Kelly

So you don't pick that same mate over and over again. That's a destructive path. I have already done it and I've only been single for three and a half years. I've seen others and I see myself do it. I step back and I'm like, OK — to not regret it means I have to learn from it and have to not do that again. So, I think that's interesting.

Faith

Well, I've had a subsequent relationship after Tim. So with my divorce with Tim and him having an affair, I feel like his decisions were about him, not so much about our life together. But about him.

During that time, now that we've been apart for 10 years, I can see that we both look at each other and think, "Oh, I could not be with that person now."

It's because we're very different. We are very, very different from when we were together. So again, it washes out. But I had a subsequent relationship after him. And I don't know about you, but dating has been very difficult for me.

I very much value monogamy and I am old fashioned. So I find someone who does not want to be monogamous with me, but wants all of the benefits. I wondered what I was lacking.

Why would that person not want just me? I mean what else could I offer? So that has been a struggle to where I withdraw from dating and I just don't want to put myself out there.

Kelly

So in that relationship, there came a time when you had to say to yourself, "I AM ENOUGH."

Faith

That's exactly what I did. I came to the conclusion that I'm better than this.

I am enough for myself that I don't need this relationship to make me whole. I can be what I rely upon.

I want someone who complements me and appreciates me because I'm going to do that for them as well. And if they don't see the value in me, then I'm not going to waste time persuading them. I shouldn't have to.

Kelly
Right. So, in both relationships, you came to a time where you had to say this and make a decision.

Faith
Right. Both were very difficult and scary. But I knew that I would, again, be more miserable staying in that situation than turning away from it.

Kelly
Give me a little background — how long were you married?

Faith
Tim and I were married for 18 years. And the last three of the 18 were pretty tumultuous. We were separated on and off for those three years.

Right after our 15th anniversary, he just decided that he didn't know if he wanted to be married. He didn't feel like this is how he wanted to live the rest of his life. Monogamy was not something he wanted to practice anymore.

I'll be honest, for a while, he tried to persuade me to have an open marriage. Again, monogamy is very important to me. The covenant of marriage is very important to me. If I just wanted to be with someone, I would not take those vows. And we just tried, he tried, to stay married.

I don't think I respected him very well after that. He was a very different person from that point on. I felt like I was living with a fraternity boy. He had just reverted back to basically the lifestyle of a 21 year old and so I lost a lot of respect for him.

And if I think something or if I feel something, you're gonna know it. I don't hide my feelings or my thoughts very well. I may not say them out loud, but you're going to feel it.

Kelly
Yes, we all feel it one way or the other.

Faith
So for the last three years, we tried that. In all honesty, I wanted to be out of the marriage. There were just so many times of me finding things and him lying.

And I just felt like I was at a standstill and I couldn't move on with my life because I made this commitment to someone that I didn't want to be with. And then, of course, the children... I wanted to keep my family together, but I didn't necessarily want to be with him.

Kelly
What happened when you finally said, "I am enough?" you Is that when you said you wanted the divorce? How did that happen?

Faith
Incrementally, I think, for me, You know, women have intuition. And I, for the first two years, I believed everything he said. Every time there was a hint of an affair, he would lie his way out of it. And I totally believed him.

But the last year, I think he was behaving in a way that was out of character for him even more. So, I think I just recognized that this is not the life that I want for myself. It's not the life I want for my children. And I started working towards doing things differently.

I went back to school. And once I started doing things that were not just for him, and not just for the children, I recognized that I'm not just a wife and I'm not just a mom, that there are other ways that I can contribute.

And there are other dreams that I had that I put to the side for so long. And it was time for me to do something about it. And I think I just gained a lot more confidence when I started doing those things.

I started finding friendships outside of my marriage. I started rekindling a lot of things that I enjoyed doing like running. I started teaching dance classes at that point. It was just a lot of things that came together.

And I had a wonderful opportunity to partner with one of my old college friends. When I was in college, we were in business school together.

He approached me about helping him with the startup company. I basically did the operations for the company and he did the sales. I was managing nursing school, children and that business and it was performing well.

It was hard but it gave me the skills and the ability to look beyond my family and to look beyond my marriage. And to see as if he wasn't there.

Because for 15 years, I was a stay at home mom and I did not work outside of the house. I didn't have anything to do with our finances. I didn't do any of it. But to know that I actually had those skills, and that I was good at it, gave me a lot of confidence to the point where that last year I started withdrawing even more so from him.

I didn't let him live at the house. I would not have sex with him. I think I just had already come to the decision that I can do this on my own. OK, I will stay because I've made the commitment to stay. But I don't have to rely on him for my happiness.

Yeah, I think that kind of carried me through the rest of my life after the divorce and now — although sometimes it's a deterrent as well for my social life because I can give off the vibe of 'she doesn't need anyone.'

Kelly
Well, it's funny, because I think you meet some men and they're attracted to that.

Faith
I am up to meet someone like that.

Kelly
And then there's a lot of men who are not like that. I've had men say, 'I like that you're so independent and you're traveling around the world, that you had your own company, and that's really attractive.'

So let's talk about kids because I know I was lucky my kids were older and they were supportive. And then I meet people or have friends who went through divorce while their kids were younger.

Can you share how young your kids were?

Faith
Yes. The boys were 13 and 14 when we got divorced, but I mean, the separation started when they were 10 and 11.

Elizabeth was tiny, she's six years younger than my middle child. It's so funny because I remember when she was little, she would make fun of Tim and me when we were being affectionate with each other. She would always comment on that and now she doesn't remember any of that. She just remembers the divorce.

But they've all been very supportive, Chris and Liam especially. I don't feel like there's any resentment with them at all toward either parent. I think they try very much to live a peaceful life with both of us.

They know why we divorced. So, they're very aware of that. And if there's any conflict between myself or Tim and them, it's things that have happened between us, not because of the divorce, at least I don't think so.

So after the divorce, Liam decided he needed to leave our hometown. He did not want to be in that small town. And so he decided to go to a private boarding school. I think that was a very good decision for him. It allowed him to start a new life where nobody knew what happened, or what we were like before. I think he needed that.

Chris is a very different person and really wanted to have the comfort and the nurturing environment that home offered. And so it was good for him to be surrounded by his family and friends. And he's also one that probably doesn't care what people think. So, you know, all of the gossip in such a small town, it didn't bother him.

And luckily, we've had some wonderful people surround us. I mean, I could not have done that without the help of my in-laws who were just amazing. We're still very close. So that really helped.

Elizabeth, on the other hand, I think holds a grudge. I think for a long time she really wanted us to get back together. I think there are times when she still feels that way. I think she probably blames me more than him for the divorce. I think she feels like I should have stuck it out and forgiven. And I have forgiven, but..

Kelly
Yeah. You forgive, you don't forget. I mean, like you said, you've become another person. In those last three years, it sounds like you were becoming another person.

Faith
Yes. Yes.

Kelly
Once you had a hold of 'her' and her badassness, you could not stay?

Faith
I agree. Tim's personality is that he enjoys having his ego stroked. He seems outwardly confident, very much so, but inwardly he's very insecure. So, he really needs someone who will tell him how wonderful he is all the time.

And I just couldn't do that for him anymore. I know that about myself. And I know that he knows that.

Kelly
You're not so wonderful if you're seeing other people. I'm not going to tell you that you are. It's hard on kids.

Faith
Yes, and I will say that they've navigated it well, with the help,

again, of the village that helped raise them. Tim and I really maintained a very good relationship, though.

Up until about three years ago, we were still having family dinners, and things were very cohesive and we co-parented well. We were helpful to each other. But in the last two or three years, it's really not that anymore.

Kelly
Well, you don't need that now.

Faith
Right. We don't need to be that. I think that helped. I think it helped the kids to adjust well to it. I think if we had been adults who badmouthed each other or could not spend time together, it would have been a different story.

Kelly
Yeah. Did you tell the kids together? Were they aware of the affairs? Did that come out? Because we sat down and told the girls together so there weren't five different stories and versions. Our therapist said we needed to do it together.

Faith
So initially, when Tim wanted to not be married, we sat the boys down together and said we were working through some things, that we wouldn't be living together and that there was a possibility of a divorce. We did not tell Elizabeth, she was only six years old at that point.

So, just until we knew for sure, we didn't want to tell her. But with the boys, they would know a difference when we weren't staying together. And Tim was traveling so much at that point, Elizabeth probably wouldn't have put two and two together.

So, fast forward. Three years later, we sat the boys down again first and let them know. And I let them know why. We didn't feel a need to hide it.

I think if that's a decision that Tim was going to make, then he was going to have to deal with the consequences of that decision.

So we told the boys first and then later that evening, had all three and let Elizabeth know. So we did tell them together. I don't know if I initially told Elizabeth why. Again, she was 9 years old at that point. We didn't go into details. But it came out later.

Kelly
I wouldn't at 9 years old either. I think that people struggle with that decision on whether to be honest about things. I know my friend Crystal had four boys and she was honest with them because the father was lying to them. And so she had to tell her truth. It's part of it.

And that's a very, very personal decision. To me, your story is so beautiful because you were able to get to that point. You did all the things you needed to do to get yourself to that point by going back to school and getting a job and giving dance lessons. I didn't know that about you. That's so cool. I love that.

Moving on to dating. Do you have any interesting lessons that you learned from dating?

Faith
I was devastated by my divorce. So it probably took me a full year before I even thought about dating.

The first guy I went out with I chose because I knew he'd just be fun. And he lived in another town at the time. He was considered a player. And so I thought well, he'll just be fun. We'll go out once and he'll forget about me.

"He reminded me of what it was like to be a woman. He was just what I needed at that time."

Because, you know, going back to not feeling like you're enough. I mean, Tim cheated on me with someone who was 20 years younger than me.

And so of course I'm going to feel like I'm not enough physically or sexually or whatever. And this particular gentleman, we had such chemistry and he made me feel so sexy and so desirable that it did wonders for my confidence.

I think that was a point in my life where I exuded confidence because he made me feel good again about myself. And I needed that. Yeah. Just little by little, you get to the point where I'm better than I thought. OK. Yeah, look at this hot shit.

But not only did he make me feel that way, he motivated me to be better. I wanted to feel good with him or without him.

So I actually started shopping again, like, actually caring about what I looked like, wearing clothes that fit me versus two sizes too big for me. I started wearing makeup again, I mean, just little things that I wasn't doing for myself because they weren't a priority. But it all came together to make me feel better about myself.

Kelly
Now, if we could just make a guy like that magically appear for every woman! I had a similar experience. And it absolutely changed how I saw myself.

I've asked everybody, "When did you make that turn and you started feeling better about yourself?" And yes, usually it is some kind of awesome, sexy relationship.

Faith

Going back to school and starting a new business, all of those things were great. They were great for me, intellectually, they were great for me, mentally, because I thought, well, I can do this and I don't need him. I can do this.

Having someone find you attractive again does wonders. We also have to have <u>our</u> egos boosted.

Kelly

After three babies and a divorce and the cheating and all of that. I mean, that's so much life. Drama, which turns to trauma, which is just hard to get past. The trauma is real for people, not just women.

Men go through it on their side too if the woman cheats. The man's feeling that too. But you know, sometimes it's not even about cheating. It's just that you grow apart. And it's sad and it's over.

Did there come a time again when you had to say "I am enough?" You said that about the dating relationship.

Faith

Yeah, I mean it's really sad that it had to be another man that made me feel that way. It's amazing. Relationships can affect you in a great way and they can affect you in a bad way. And not just with your partner that you had your children, I mean, we put so much into those relationships.

For me, I expect a lot out of those relationships as well. And not everybody can fulfill those expectations.

So going back to the thought of gratitude, you know, being grateful for those times when those expectations are met or exceeded in those relationships and not dwelling on when they aren't — this is very key for me.

In life in general, it's really easy to have a poor outlook on the world. And I struggled in the last couple of years with COVID and how people were behaving. I was very disappointed and I hope that I'm coming out of that and really looking at the good in people again. I do want to see that. I think that makes the difference between a happy life and a sad life.

Kelly

Absolutely. I feel like the older I get, the more examples I see of people being gracious and having gratitude that are just so inspiring. It makes me want to pay more attention.

Sometimes I feel that little irritation or frustration and I say, OK, well, maybe they're having a bad day. I'm not having a bad day. So maybe I can just smile at them.

And I feel grateful that I have the heart to take a step back and let them have their moment. And I've had a lot of good lessons recently from my moving and traveling.

While traveling, people can get funky and tired and nasty. And to just keep that smile on my face and just be grateful, grateful that I'm here. I'm in Italy, so I'm not gonna let them ruin my day. And I'm gonna smile at you and hopefully make your day even though you have no idea what I'm saying.

Faith

I just think living as long as we have and going through the things that we've gone through, we can put it in perspective. And say, you know what, this is really not a big deal. So just smile and let it go.

But then stand firm on the things that are a big deal.

Kelly

Do you feel like there's been red flags that you missed? Like in dating? Because I'm looking and thinking about the patterns.

Faith

So Kelly, I'm horrible in that I'm attracted to the wrong men. I'm attracted to the quiet confident type. But generally, those confident, strong men tend to have really big egos.

And it's been in my face the last few weeks, whether it be in conversations or on the news, or the little Instagram posts talking about being the person that you want to attract.

Kelly

Yep. And?

Faith

I am looking inward and that maybe I'm the one with the big ego, because I attract these people. So maybe I need to look at myself and see what I'm doing and maybe I should make some adjustments in my life. Because I want someone who's warm and kind and honest and has good character. I want those things. So I need to be those things.

Kelly

That's it. I just finished a 49-day workshop. And this was kind of the end of the workshop. But she had us make a list of what we wanted in a partner. And that came up to 19 things.

And then she said pick five and I did. And then she instructed me to go be those things in the world so that you can attract them. Exactly what you said is what the whole premise is.

And I think here I am 56 years old and hearing this for the first time. But I heard it.

OK, so these questions are a little bit easier, I think.

What feeds your soul now? Like what gives you satisfaction or goodness?

Faith
You know what? Family is always going to be first for me. I am empty nesting for the first time. So, in all honesty, what feeds my soul is time with those that I love most in this world.

And that would be those three. I am happiest when I get to spend lunch with them or just watching them. Yeah, that feeds my soul.

But apart from that, I think I'm still trying to figure that out. I am in a weird phase right now in that I actually have time to do some of those things. I'm not waiting on someone to come home for dinner. And you know, my schedule isn't wrapped around kids.

I'm actually finding that I have spaces to fill. And so even though I enjoy running and spending time with friends, and really just enjoy being at home, I need to find other outlets. So I wish I could.

Kelly
One of the things I write about in this book is that I used the app Meetup and found hiking groups and people that were interested in learning swing dancing, and I went crazy on meetups and I met all kinds of people. But it was fun. It was fun to hike. You like to dance.

I like to dance. And I went out and I took salsa lessons and I even found them for free on Meetup.

Faith

I need to do that! I need to try.

Kelly

OK, next question. When you get sad or you're having a bad day, what do you do to self soothe? What do you do to keep yourself calm and keep peace in your life?

Faith

I probably do three things. I pray. I will listen to music and I run. I mean, those really are the three things that if I'm having a bad day, that's what I will do. And generally, they help me through that day, because I have them. I have days of feeling alone or feeling unappreciated.

Make that four things. You know, what I really love to do is go through my photos. Yeah. Because it helps me to remember good times and be grateful.

Kelly

Oh, I love that. That's a great tip. Love that. What are you hopeful for?

Faith

Hopeful. Gosh, I'm hopeful for a few things. Recently, I guess what I'm concentrating on is finding purpose again. For a long time, I felt like my purpose was being a mom and doing all of those things while my kids were in the house.

And now this is gonna sound really hokey. OK. So I went to nursing school not thinking my marriage is going to end. I went to nursing school because I wanted to do medical missions. I didn't even think that I would be working full time. I just thought, well, I'll work part time, PRN, and go on medical missions.

And then, we went through the divorce and I had to work. I've had to have income.

And now I'm going back to the idea of medical missions again. I think it's something that God's put into my heart that I want to fulfill. So it's odd that you asked that question, because, as of this morning, I was applying for mission trips.

Kelly
Hokey? Don't say that! I love it. That's awesome.

Well, what we are doing here and now is me. I've been wanting to write forever and here I am. This is my hopeful. Yes. I hope that I help somebody, even if I help one person. It's also helping me to talk to everybody about this. And then you lift it up, lift it up with all of them.

Faith
I'm also hopeful that I'll find a partner. Yes. I'm hopeful that he will come into my life soon and then I'll be able to share my children with him and my grandchildren. Very hopeful for that.

Kelly
Last question. Any last advice for people going through a big change in their life?

Faith
It's hard. It sucks at times. I mean, I remember not seeing the light at the end of the tunnel. But there is one. And it's very cliche to say

that at some point in your life, you will look back and be grateful for it.

"So be grateful for those hard moments because they've made you who you are. And when you figure out that you are enough — and that you're not just enough — you're pretty great. It's all worth it."

Empowerment Practice 2: Make a Resume of Your Life

This chapter is all about your worth. Some of us have been at-home moms. Some have had amazing careers. Some of us have lived a sweet, small-town life that was everything we had dreamed of. Many of us however have had hardship. And some of us are hurting like hell right now. I've been there.

But we have ALL accomplished things in our lives. Accomplishments don't make us who we are and they are not our purpose. Your purpose is the impact you want to make on the world.

We have probably all had to build a resume at some point and we list all of our work accomplishments. But what about what you are called to do — then and now. I believe if you look back at your non-work life, you will see how your past actions can show you your purpose.

I challenge you to open a blank document on your laptop or grab a clean piece of paper and do the following.

1. Write one sentence about what you want for yourself. For example, *With all I have learned in my life, I am going to be an amazing non-profit leader, a faithful and kind partner and the best grandma ever seen.*

2. Make bullet points with high level statements about your deeply personal accomplishments in life. List what makes

you happy when you reminisce. This isn't about business. This is about emotions and love. For example:

- o I raised three incredibly talented, empathetic, loving and fun daughters.
- o I built a loving household where my friends and family felt welcome.
- o I entertained and put a smile on many people's faces.
- o I ran nine half marathons and was in the best shape of my life at 50.
- o I served on non-profit boards and made a difference in the community.

3. Now go back and put two or three small bullets under each of the topics. What did you do that you are proud of? How did you accomplish these things? Keep it simple. If it makes you smile, write it down. For example,

- o I served on non-profit boards and made a difference in the community.
  - I helped the child advocacy center raise money to help abused children.
  - I gathered silent auction items for the fundraiser for the youth choir summer tour.
  - I wrote marketing pieces for the historic preservation nonprofit which helped them raise awareness and raise funds.
- o I raised three incredibly talented, empathetic, loving and fun daughters.
  - I showed up at every game or match or dance recital that was possible.
  - I made a place where their friends would want to come and play.

- I included them in family traditions like making Scottish oatcakes at Christmas.
- I showed them tough love when they needed it.
- I was there and I still am, when they need me. Anytime.

As you do this exercise, my hope is that you will see that all the little things you did in life add up to big things. They just might guide you to your future purpose.

Whatever has happened in your life that brought you to this book, nothing can take away all of the amazing things you have done in your life.

The smallest things: They are worthy of your remembrance. May they bring you joy.

YOUR NEW LIFE IS GOING TO COST YOU YOUR OLD ONE.
IT'S GOING TO COST YOU YOUR COMFORT ZONE
AND YOUR SENSE OF DIRECTION.
IT'S GOING TO COST YOU RELATIONSHIPS AND FRIENDS.
IT'S GOING TO COST YOU BEING LIKED AND UNDERSTOOD.
BUT IT DOESN'T MATTER.

BECAUSE THE PEOPLE WHO ARE MEANT FOR YOU
ARE GOING TO MEET YOU ON THE OTHER SIDE.
AND YOU'RE GOING TO BUILD A NEW COMFORT ZONE AROUND THE
THINGS THAT ACTUALLY MOVE YOU FORWARD.
AND INSTEAD OF LIKED, YOU'RE GOING TO BE LOVED.
INSTEAD OF UNDERSTOOD, YOU'RE GOING TO BE SEEN.
ALL YOU'RE GOING TO LOSE IS WHAT WAS BUILT FOR A PERSON YOU
NO LONGER ARE. LET IT GO.

THE MINDS JOURNAL.COM| **BRIANNA WEST**

CHAPTER 3:
FIGHT FOR IT — OR NOT

At some point in everyone's life, there is a life-changing decision that must be made. When a crisis comes, that is usually a 'given' circumstance. The crisis may be born out of your own mistakes or other's choices. It may be born out of death or a different type of goodbye.

Some married people choose to stay together during and after a crisis through hard work and loving each other 'through it.' Some people choose to move on outside their marriage (during or after). Then there are the unconventional couples who stay together but shift to an open marriage. Some just feel stuck — lost and forgotten within the marriage, but without a plan.

All of these situations likely cause strife of some type and certainly some deep soul searching.

After three years of feeling lost and alone within my own marriage, I hit a breaking point. I could not take the loneliness anymore. To this day I remember the exact date even though it is eight years later.

My husband came home from work and I asked him to sit down at the kitchen table. I was terrified to have this discussion, but I was way more terrified NOT to have it.

I asked him if he was happy. He shrugged his shoulders and just looked at me.

I mustered up my courage and shared that I had been going to a marriage counselor by myself for a few weeks.

I said, "I'm unhappy — very unhappy. I think about leaving you every day, multiple times a day. I feel so alone. In fact, when you are home, I feel lonelier than when you are out of town."

I went on to say we either needed to go to counseling together or I needed to leave. I shared with him that although he claimed he wasn't having an affair, I could think of no other reason for his change in behavior. I just couldn't take the blank look in his eyes anymore.

I was standing by the kitchen table, gripping the tops of two of the chairs, shaking like a leaf. This was one of the scariest moments of my life. I had been fighting for my marriage and I badly needed him to get back in the arena with me.

When I look back, I can see mistakes I made in that conversation. The most important one is what I'd like you to take away.

When you come to a conversation like this in your life, don't work to fill the void. Let the silence do its job by creating space for the other person to share. I didn't do that very well, so learn from me.

After that painful and vulnerable conversation, he agreed that night to go to counseling. He said he loved me and wanted to work it out. We went for months working on communication, our sex life and working through disagreements about the caretaking plan for a family member who had sustained an injury and would need permanent care.

Our relationship did temporarily get better, but I still felt on edge. I still felt like I couldn't feel the love we once had.

For example, at one point in early 2016, we both had a health challenge, my hip and his shoulder. We had to spend extended periods of time taking care of each other at home in what we called our 'geriatric ward.' It actually felt like the old us — the team.

Eventually, though, I felt him drifting away again. And sadly, I continued to buy into the idea it was my fault. I continued to feel like I was the one who had to change and I tried and I tried and I tried.

As you now know, it ended in divorce.

Shania Interview

While these shifts in my marriage were happening, our dear friends were also going through a rough patch. I want to introduce you to Shania and let her share their story of courage, vulnerability and love — and how they made their marriage work.

Kelly

I've been asking everybody to give their background. Some start professionally and some people start back in childhood. It's up to you.

Shania

I'd love to start in my childhood. Shout out to my mother, because really, my childhood influenced my adulthood. I mean, it does for all of us, and you can choose how much it influences you, or the way it influences you, but it's going to influence you.

I had a great childhood up until middle school. My parents were together. My mom stayed at home. She dedicated herself to us — not in a bad way. Now it's crazy how people have gone overboard with how much time they invest in their children. But that's another interview!

I started out with a solid foundation that every kid deserves. I had love when I needed it. I had a home. I had food. We weren't rich, but I didn't have to worry about anything. All of my needs were met.

I watched my parents together, but I didn't really watch them have this relationship where you would say, "That's what I want to be when I grow up."

But they also weren't the relationship where you would say, "I'm not going to be that way when I grow up."

They were neither so that was kind of a neutral area.

Then our lives changed a lot in middle school when they divorced. Other things happened in life, but still we did have a good start. I want to share the good start and share my experience with their divorce because it impacted me.

I can remember not thinking or worrying about their relationship. I think that's also something every kid deserves — not to worry about the parents, especially when they're that young.

I remember them sitting us on the couch, me and my two sisters, and usually when we're on the couch, we're in trouble. Like we've done something — we've broken a lamp or something.

Kelly
You thought, "We're in trouble, they found the lamp."

Shania
Exactly. But what they said was they were getting divorced and because we hadn't thought about it, I was floored. I was just completely confused because I had no clues about this.

Generally, they really hid their conflicts from us. I'm not really sure how I feel about that, like when you're in elementary school you don't really want to think about it. But I just remember being floored and not really feeling like I understood why it happened.

But they gave us a good divorce.

And they maintained that same parenting relationship they had together after the divorce. For example, we would have dinner with my dad quite often. And that was as good of a divorce as you can get.

I have never been one of the people who was overly optimistic that I'm gonna be married forever. But if I don't make it, I want to give my kids a good divorce. I mean, it sounds like a gift. I'm giving you a good divorce.

I had a little bit of animosity about not knowing that anything was going on because everybody wants that prep, you know. It was a shock and yet it wasn't a shock because they weren't really showing each other they love each other.

I remember one time my parents kissing and it was a peck — once. So I didn't see at least the physical. They supported each other, you know, but my dad worked a lot. My mom was at home.

But you mentioned professional background as well. I consider myself to have had four careers in my life. The first one was nursing. And that was when I was younger.

I did not go through life intentionally. I just went through life. And really that's changed only recently.

So for a very big part of my life. I was floating through it, not dragging myself through it. You have to pick a career. And I thought oh, maybe I'd like to be a doctor and when I went to school, I realized the classes are really hard. Maybe I'll be a nurse instead.

The classes were hard. It was microbiology!

Kelly

My biology class was so early my freshman year.

Shania

Me too! How can you do that? And why?

Kelly

Why <u>did</u> we do that? Because nobody told us! We're the oldest.

Shania

I think we did it because we're freshmen and the freshmen get all the early classes. I didn't know any better.

So my first thought was nursing. I loved it. I loved helping people.

I was a nursing assistant for three years before I was a nurse. I loved having that relationship with a patient where we talked about vulnerability in the hospital. Those patients are vulnerable and I love just being able to be present with people in those moments.

Most of my nursing assistant time was on a surgical floor. And then as a nurse, I was in cardiac intensive care and later I moved to surgery. And so that was my first career.

Then I got pregnant. I went back to work after my first kid, but then we moved to California and I stopped working.

I had no intention to stop working. I had no intention that I wanted to be that homemaker. I just hadn't thought it out because I was just going through life. I was not driving [my life].

When we moved it was hard because we're alone at home. My husband Vince was gone two months, home two months. There wasn't a place for me to work except an hour's drive away. It was inconvenient so I gave up working and that lasted a long time.

And then I was 'just' a mom. I would say mom/volunteer because that's what you do. But I loved it. I loved being with the kids and I look at that as a career just as important as my nursing career. It was great.

Kelly

Exactly. If I put all my volunteering on my resume, it would be 20 pages long. And it 'doesn't count.' And I'm putting that in quotes!

Shania

No, it doesn't. It's funny.

Kelly

I raised so much money for churches, athletic teams, schools — all of it.

Shania

It's amazing. Because I remember I was talking to Vince about retirement. He said, "Yeah, I'm gonna volunteer when I retire" and I said, "I put in all my volunteer work already."

And he said, "When did you volunteer?"

I said, "Are you serious?"

I ran soccer tournaments. I was a room mom. Working every book fair and in the library. All the volunteering around the child was done by me.

And then I went back to school.

Kelly

Going back to school was when your kids were in high school?

Shania

Yeah. I went back to school to get my master's in library science.

And I think you started going back to work when the kids were a little older.

Kelly
I went back to work in 2008.

Shania
I think that was probably the same time I was getting started again on another chapter of my life.

Earlier we were discussing supporting people and finding an answer to a question. You said the question in your head for the Camino was basically: How do you pivot? How do you go on? How do you start over?

I thought about finding [a new] career and going back to school. It was not easy for me to go back to school, especially at 40 years old, a husband at home and kids — because your brain just stopped working the academic way. You know you are using your brain, just not the academic way.

Kelly
In school, you focus on one thing, or maybe two different classes, but you're focusing on one thing — school. Yeah, as a Mom, you're focusing on 20 things at once.

Shania
Definitely. But academics is a different route. And so getting back into the habits was a little scary, but also fun.

That's the first time I coined the phrase 'my brain hurts' because you're thinking so hard, there is a sensation and it's really hard to describe, but just trying to think so hard.

Anyway, that was the question on my path. What would life look like on my own if this relationship didn't work?

That was at the beginning of this year in my life, when I said to myself, "OK, I've been hanging on to everybody's coattails."

I had been floating down the river with everybody else for 40 years and I realized that I was letting other peoples' currents drive me.

I really wanted to decide which way I was gonna go in the river and put my paddle in the river, not just be sitting back. Because it took that long to see what happens when you're not participating in your direction.

It wasn't easy. I am applying for college again now to get a second master's degree. I was going through the list of questions that they asked and one was, "What hardships have you overcome to get here today?"

And I thought, "OK, this is not right for a 51 year old."

I know that would take all day! Anybody has hardships, even in work, and I'm so lucky to be here. That's why I wanted to start in childhood.

I feel like I have had what I needed my whole life until I was 40 and that I needed to decide — What do I need now?

So I had a career as a librarian and I loved that. I still love it. It was really hard to let it go when I did. And my fourth career I went into project management for web developers.

It started out with design, which was a really interesting space, especially that world of computers and everything's changing so fast all the time. The rapid change in that business never slows down.

Kelly
OK, thank you so much for that background. So, how long have you been married now to Vince?

Shania
27 years. How long were you married?

Kelly
31 years. What are the characteristics that you love and enjoy about your husband?

Shania
So his intellect is number one. I just love how he's just really smart, smarter than me. He just remembers things and it's like having a human dictionary or encyclopedia around, which is really cool. And Vince values education, which is probably why he has all those thoughts in his head.

That probably was what attracted me to him the most, but also his sense of humor. He's got that whole dad humor going. And that's just the thing, it doesn't have to be super legitimately funny to make me laugh.

That's one thing I wanted in a relationship because I can remember the relationships I had beforehand. Humor had to be there and you had to laugh and to get along in my family. You have to laugh because if you're not laughing, you're just really probably feeling very uncomfortable because that's all we do.

I don't know if this is an attribute, but it's his love language. And that is cooking. He loves his cooking! So to have a husband who loves cooking is, yeah, that's hot. Honestly.

Kelly
What are the differences about you that actually helped?

Shania
I think the biggest differences that make our relationship work are about how we attack the world.

I say yes to anything. I mean, you can just tell from my career path. And to the people who read this book — don't take advantage of me — because I will say yes to anything.

So I say yes to everything. He says no to everything.

He's very cautious. I just went on this big trip where we are gonna be in the woods with a backpack, not alone but with a group and in a foreign country. My niece and I went through planning our trip not even thinking about the bad things that could happen.

And then before I left, he said, "Have you thought about this? Have you thought about that?"

You know, it helps me prepare because I'm a dreamer. I'm just thinking let's go do, let's go have the adventure.

And so it causes friction between us because we've had to deal with each other to such extremes, but it really helps ground me and I count on that. And I can help give him some perspective. I don't use it all the time but it definitely gives me valuable information.

Kelly

Are there characteristics that can cause conflict? I can see this causing good and bad.

Shania

Yeah, it probably causes as much conflict as it doesn't. Let's see. What are the characteristics that caused the most conflict? Yeah, you might know since you're my complaining ear.

Kelly

Well, I think there are fundamental life choices. I mean, we both went through our husbands not wanting us to go to church.

Shania

We've been able to settle into a rhythm where if I say yes and he says no, we just respect each other, and I say yes with somebody else. Not another man though.

For example, I ask him if he wants to hike and he says no, I go hiking with a friend.

We don't hold that against each other. I may pout a little bit, but I don't hold it against him. That's just nature. This is mine and I'm OK with that because I can still feed myself.

I know we've had this conversation before that I feel like we put too much pressure on our relationships to be everything. I have seen some couples who are [each other's] everything and I'm so happy for them. But I think in general, people are so nuanced, we cannot expect everything from each other.

There are deal breakers because you have two people and each of you have your needs. What are the needs that you absolutely must have filled by your spouse? Then what are the other ones? Don't ignore them, but find other outlets, as long as it's not sex. Because that's the deal breaker.

Kelly
So now we're gonna talk about religion.

Shania
I think it's definitely a source of contention and definitely, when we met, we were kind of on the same page because I grew up without any religion at all. And he grew up with a very strict religion. And so we came together and really didn't have a path.

And then later in life, I found my path within Christianity that really fed my soul and that was one thing that I wanted to share with him. And that was one thing for him that he didn't want me to have or to share with him because of his upbringing.

So that was one difference in needs that we had. We were not respecting each other's view on it. Maybe respecting it, but not supporting it. So I think that's probably it.

This was coming to a head. We were having a hard time. Because I was really involved in the church and he really didn't want me to be. I think eventually we came to try to respect each other, but there was always a tension behind it. He doesn't want this for me.

Kelly
That is a perfect segue.

At some points in your marriage, you had a rough patch. You went back to school thinking what does it look like if I'm on my own? You were at the point you were thinking this and then the religion thing was contentious.

With that rough patch, I mean, we all have more than one. But that one was hard for you guys. And you took steps? Whatever you want to share about that would be helpful.

Shania

Well, I think there were probably a couple of years where we really drifted apart. We had really never established good communication. Like with everything else, we fell into letting each other do our things. We really didn't intentionally communicate with each other.

So you drift apart and then all of a sudden you're at this place where I'm looking at him going, "Who is this person? This is not the person I married."

And I think a lot of people say that. I think you grow and you get to where you aren't the same person for them.

Kelly

I think that's an important statement. Because it's a fact that we change. In fact, we can change every day. And if your expectation is for your partner to stay that person, you are setting yourself up for disappointment.

Shania

Absolutely. But I think when I said that statement, I completely want to clarify — I didn't choose to be with a person who acted the way he was acting. I'm sure he was saying the same about me because we were not being nice to each other.

You know how you are when you wake up on the wrong side of bed? You didn't sleep well. Everything's going wrong. You have an interaction with somebody and you're just cranky.

Kelly

And the cranky begets the cranky begets the cranky, it's just that law of attraction. If you're putting out cranky, you're getting cranky back.

Shania

I remember one of our walks and I remember a conversation that we had. Afterwards I remember thinking, "I know he can be another way for me."

Should I just let him be another way for somebody else? Or should I change this so he's that way for me? Because I just knew if we got divorced he was going to go be that nice person again. I knew it.

I could see him being that way with other people. I knew he was still there and that we had just gotten in this rut and we couldn't be there for each other because we weren't communicating.

We were just letting ourselves slide down to where we were on the edge of the cliff.

I remember one day when I'd had it. He'd had it. I know we were both at the point where we were thinking this isn't the way I want to live.

We got in the car and went for a drive. I have always felt that tough conversations are great to have in the car. You can't escape. You can't leave and you don't have to look each other in the eye because somebody's driving. So it's taking that pressure off the intensity of the conversation. And it's just a small space.

It's providing everything you need to force a conversation, which is sad. You shouldn't have to force it, but we did. We weren't communicating well. And I used it with my teenagers sometimes too because they never want to look you in the eye.

Anyway, on our drive, I just remember the anger left me. And I think it left him too.

We were facing it and we both realized our marriage was broken. And I think he thought it was irretrievable. I kind of wondered if it was irretrievable.

This is the thing that I always throw out. I know I've said it to you a million times.

I said, "We need to leave it all on the field. We haven't tried. There are stones that have not been turned over yet."

I think he fought back a little bit when I said that.

For every really big problem that I've had, I will dissect it and I say, "Take a step back. What is the problem to solve? What is the core? What's the promise?"

We decided to go to a counselor. Going to a counselor, you're committing to be vulnerable for an hour for somebody. If you're not, then you might as well not go. I think that was a hard decision to make.

I felt like finding somebody that we could trust — it had to be somebody that he would respect. I found somebody and he ended up being just lovely. What he did for us is he taught us to communicate.

We were in counseling for probably a year or more. I think we stopped when I went back to school because I had a conflict with my hours and I couldn't go during that time.

I remember thinking, I don't want to stop — will that mean he can't communicate with me now? Even though it had continuity, we're still mainly communicating in that hour. As time went on, it bled out a little, but I was still really nervous. To not have that person that said you could do it, building skills for you.

There were two things that were instrumental in changing. One of them came from your in-laws.

Kelly
Oh I know what it is! "You could be right."

Shania
Yes! Because when you have somebody super smart, they really are right 95 percent of the time. But give me my 5 percent please.

So I know he really, really wanted to say he was right. So having that phrase [you could be right] that he could just say was fantastic.

And then the other thing that our counselor taught him is what to do when you come in the door from work. Because, you know, if you're staying at home, your husband's working, you have a long day with kids, they have a long day at work. My expectation when he came in was to help!

Kelly
Well, that's the whole premise behind the book by John Gray, <u>Men Are from Mars, Women Are from Venus.</u>

Shania
Yeah. So our counselor said every day when you come home, come in and give your wife a kiss.

Doesn't matter how you feel, come in and give her a kiss. And at first, that kiss is going to feel really forced. But eventually, it's going to turn into what it is now.

It's bringing tears to my eyes because sometimes now he just comes in from the other room and gives me a kiss.

And to me, he's saying, "I'm committed to you and I'm glad you're in this room."

And wow, two things. Two little things made such a huge difference in our relationship.

We were at a place where we could have said no. And in the end, the only reason we didn't wasn't because I said oh, 'all you need to do is give me a kiss' and say 'you could be right.'

Because we looked at the problem and we said, "How does this need to be solved or no, it's unsolvable." And it turns out it was solvable for us.

Kelly
That's beautiful.

When you were going through that counseling and he's teaching you to communicate, you said you loved that hour. And it's probably because you're being vulnerable. Were you still cranky at home?

Shania
Oh, yeah. It was a transition from cranky over a year but there were definitely some times I can remember those kisses at the beginning being still cranky, but really the kiss went so far. This wasn't a big emotional, passionate kiss. This is just "I'm home."

And to me it meant, "I'm trying for you. You're worth trying for."

Kelly

What was it like for you and your kids and your husband at that time? Were they aware of the tension?

Shania

They were, I think. It's funny. I brought up the relationship with my parents and that I had a little animosity toward them because of me not knowing about their divorce before they dropped it on us.

But I really did want to protect the kids from what we were going through. People are cranky together. So I know that they had to know mom and dad weren't doing well.

I just wanted our kids to live their little lives and not know. I knew that if there was a time when that wasn't gonna happen, that we were going to have to start having those conversations. I'm really ambivalent about this because as a kid I wanted to at least have some kind of clue from our parents. Now I'm saying when we're giving clues, it was bad. They were like 14 and 11 and to me, that still felt young.

Kelly

How were you feeling about yourself during this time?

Shania

I was feeling vulnerable. I've been sitting at home for years and years and years.

And I felt like if this goes south, I am in a position where I can't support myself. And I was mad at myself because I felt like I let myself get in that position.

My mom always told me to be an independent woman and she drove it home. She was from the generation of women's lib. But I just went along the river and I let myself be in a position where I was not an independent woman.

I think it's OK to not be independent. But I just wish I had worked as a nurse twice a month or something like that. I was to the point where I couldn't go back to nursing without a hassle because the license had expired.

There were just no prospects for me. I am an independent woman now, but at the time, I felt dependent and I felt vulnerable.

I think that there were lots of options, but you get there and it's like deer in the headlights. Your life trajectory changes and is not where you were and you've got to think about this.

Because to be an independent woman, you have to be guiding your life, and I wasn't.

Kelly
Do you continually reassess your marriage now, either of you? Do both of you do it together. Do you do a check in or something like that?

Shania
I wish I could say I do that with him, but I don't. But I do that for myself.

We talked at the beginning of the conversation about how we all change and big things really change people. Going back to school, being a librarian, being in a different area, it all changes who you are and who you want to be.

The other thing that changes is your life stage. I feel like the other pressure that we put on each other as spouses is assuming we should be perfect at every stage of life. We can't be spouses together like before kids when you have that relationship that is just you two. You have kids and it's requiring a different role for each person. You have to be a partnership.

Kelly
Before you have a romance and now you have to be a partner.

Shania
Exactly. And you have a different role, a mom and a dad, that's a whole different role from being a spouse. At each stage in our relationship, I thought, is this a good stage for us?

After the kids left, I remember that was the biggest time where I've thought, "Is this working? Are we a couple and is this working at this stage of our life?"

I was really nervous about it, but it's been great. It's been so good. It's a little different than the honeymoon period, because you're in your 20s and you have all your energy. You have your different things.

So it's different and it's lovely.

Now we're kind of looking at retirement and I'm just doing the same thing. I'm evaluating how we are going to be as a couple in retirement because that's a whole different way of looking at it.

I am continually evaluating and I don't know if that's because I felt vulnerable earlier in our marriage. I want to know what the next stage is. We're trying to talk about it, but before it would just be in our own heads.

Kelly

Yeah. What do you do specifically now to just stay happy?

Shania

Me personally? Well, I like my work. It makes me happy. We've talked about retirement, but I'm saying, no, I like this work. This is fun.

I do think maybe me having that perspective of staying at home and not being in the workforce for so long — it gave me that extra pizzazz.

Kelly

Yeah, I think when I went back to work, it was so exciting. Yeah, it was scary, but it was fun and it was something that was mine. I was able to give of myself in a completely different way. So it was still about giving. It was still about doing for others. But in a way it was that thing to keep me happy.

Shania

And I think that what you just said is really more than independent. It's about having something that is yours. So I really do get a lot of happiness from work and then obviously from hiking.

Something about going into the woods and just being in nature because I think that at my core that I'm probably just a person who likes "to be" and that's why I let the river take me for so long. So directing my life is work for me. And hiking is just being in that moment.

Kelly

And it's a connection that is almost like you are unaware you're connecting with nature. You're having a conversation with yourself in your head. You have time to connect with your words, your desires, your wants or what you don't want — even your fears. Hiking allows for connection within and that is, I guess, the same thing as being still.

If you can't be still, are you ever going to know what you want, know what you need, know who you are?

Shania
I think that's an important distinction because not everybody can hike. There's been times in my life due to physical limitations that I couldn't hike.

Kelly
This is where it's important to find something you can do. I've been thinking about trying tai chi when I can't do yoga anymore. And meditation is there and it's available to anyone.

Shania
It is and I think it's easier to be still in meditation.

Kelly
I'm meditating while I'm walking, but it was a skill I had to develop.

Shania
I think the benefit that I get from hiking is obviously this activity.

Kelly
Everybody needs to find the ability to get through the roadblocks that are just hanging out there and need to be dealt with. I feel like sometimes we beat those thoughts to death.

Shania
Yes, the spins are bad. It's like the spin cycle. You've got to stop.

Kelly

That's why I need people. I need to walk with a friend. There's nothing to replace it, but even walking by yourself helps because then you realize that you've thought this to death. There's nothing new that can come out of these thoughts.

And you can just put it back on the shelf. You can say it's done. Sometimes it's an epiphany and sometimes it needs more time. It's like leaving it all on the field for that thought, that instance. Then for me, it's still there and it's going to poke me until I give it the time it deserves.

Yeah, and most of the time, it's just poking you when you're trying to sleep.

You and another person said to me that I process best by just saying it out loud and saying it out loud to someone I trust. Yes, you're being vulnerable. But what it does is it takes the scariness out of it. A lot of the time it didn't sound as bad out loud as it did in my head.

Shania

Yeah, I think it takes a different brainpower to think something than it does to say it out loud because you have to say it in a way that the person is going to understand. And sometimes just finding the words to say it to another person makes me understand it better.

Kelly

You find your own answer. That's the key to therapy. They just get you to say it out loud.

The last four questions I'm asking everyone. What feeds your soul?

Shania

I think people feed my soul. Like being with you. And to just be with my family.

Sometimes I feel my energy drop and I just call them. I'll just call my dad and have that phone conversation.

That connection of being around people feeds my soul. Honestly, when I think about what I need, what my soul needs in life, that's probably all it needs.

Kelly

So we all have bad times. What do you do to self soothe?

Shania

I'll read and I'll take a nap. That's where I'm rejuvenated.

Kelly

What are you hopeful for?

Shania

I am just hopeful that I have 20 years of living. Because I feel like every time I turn around, there's something else really cool. I'm really excited about our next trip that we're planning, but I just really am hopeful that I keep seeing the really cool things in life and keep having the ability to say yes.

Kelly

Last one, what advice do you have for people going through a big change?

Shania

I think taking a step back and looking at the big picture is really important. We can get sucked into details easily. And I think that's why communication with your people is so helpful. But you know what, I know that not everybody has people — that is a gift. And some of it is luck.

I think other people give us that big picture perspective because they're not stuck in the details of what's going on. And it's so refreshing to talk to you about all the hard times in a relationship.

I think the biggest thing you can do is to step back, look at the big picture and say, "What is the problem?"

Part of this is sometimes you have to ask yourself a few times to get to the real problem. You know, sometimes it'll be, "He's not talking to me."

And then you have to take another step back and then another step back.

For example, during my career change. What do I know? Why am I doing this? What is at the heart of my next career change?

And when you do that, it can provide fuel for the answers. It can also make you more open to see different directions because people get caught up on what they're supposed to do because of the way they're viewing the problem.

But if you step back, you might see that there are more ways to solve your problem than what you're thinking because you've reframed the problem.

Kelly
You're making me think about 2021 when I was trying to envision what I would do after I fulfill my three years with the company I was working with and my contract would be over. I thought there was a possibility they were gonna say, 'Hey, we're done with you.'

But on the other hand, I had the freedom to say, "Hey, I'm done with you."

I was trying to envision what I could do and so I was thinking I'm gonna get to the beach. I start thinking "I'm going to sell my house and downsize and then I'm gonna buy something at the beach."

And here's the deal....that was probably iteration number seven of what I had dreamed for myself but I finally was able to start picturing myself out of this hometown — out of this place. And what I started seeing, because I stood back, was that I was in a cage. I was in the cage of my old life.

I was stuck in that cage partly because I had this responsibility to the company that bought my company, but part of it was also I was still trying to make a home for everyone. I was still trying to hold that part of it together.

And in the meantime, I try to start a new life. But until I stepped back I only thought, "I gotta keep working, I gotta save for retirement. I have to."

This is what everybody does. You work until you're 65.

And what if I don't have to do that? What if I take two years off? All of a sudden, I opened the door of that cage.

Shania
I know I have felt trapped and when I am able to take a step back, I can see I feel trapped because I don't think I have options A, B and C.

Or maybe you feel completely trapped because there's only ABC.

But when you take a step back and you look up, you know what is the big picture here. You know what is gonna bring you happiness. Then you can see the broader picture beyond, "I need that piece of chocolate cake."

Kelly
Of course you're gonna say something about chocolate.

Shania
It's gonna come up eventually. Right? I've thought about it three times during this interview. Yeah, I was gonna say hot chocolate to self soothe, but I've had to give it up lately.

I wish that there was a better example of seeing the big picture but that's what it is.

And sometimes it's hard to see yourself. That's why it's really nice to have that sounding board to say that you need something different.

Maybe you'll just see if you take a step back, you'll just see the bigger picture, and I think it's just freeing. It's when you say, see the bigger picture, you're out of that cage, you're not trapped anymore and you think differently.

Kelly
Yeah, when I finally thought well, what if I buy a condo outside Savannah, Georgia? I think that led me down the path of seeing myself not in Nashville anymore. And I think that doesn't make everybody in my life happy — that I'm not there.

I miss out on things. I miss people. Maybe I'll be back, but it's what is right for me right now.

I'm able to grow. I can feel things. It's just an incredible opportunity that I've manifested here.

Shania

I know. I feel like you're on an adventure.

Kelly

Yeah, I think that's the best part of all of it. It is an adventure. It doesn't feel like a cage.

Empowerment Practice 3: Take a Step Back

Shania has given us some powerful advice. When we are in the heat of the battle, it can be difficult to see the core of the problem. When the pain is blinding, I daresay, it is near impossible.

What if we could let the pain or the situation sit beside us like an old friend? Just the thought of that is quite powerful to me.

Let's go a step further name the situation. Not death, divorce, infidelity, or failure.

Let's call it Friend. Friend is a peaceful presence and it cannot hurt you. And because it does not have the power to hurt you, you can say anything to Friend.

Get a piece of paper and pen or have a blank document open on your computer. Be ready to write after the exercise.

1. Close your eyes, in a quiet and safe place take three long slow deep breaths so that you are ready for meditation. If you cannot calm your mind, just say, "Hello!" out loud. This was a technique given by Michael Singer in *The Untethered Soul: A Journey Beyond Yourself* and it works for me.

   Say hello as many times as you need until that voice in your head is quiet.

2. When you are quiet and relaxed, say hello to Friend. Tell Friend how this situation has made you feel.

3. Now define for Friend the struggle you are facing. Your goal here is to name the core problem or challenge.

4. Now, it's time to turn the tables. Now you are Friend. Advize yourself on how to take the first step toward resolving the core problem. Could there be another way to view this?

5. When you have reached this point, write down your experience. Define the feelings, the problem and the first step toward solution. Can you say, "You could be right"?

My experience is when you name the problem and you say out loud what it is to experience the emotions related to the problem, it takes the power away from the situation.

If you name it and call it what it is, you are taking back your power. As long as the core problem is ruling your mind, the problem has your power.

Take your power back now.

"SOMETIMES YOU HAVE TO WALK AWAY FROM PEOPLE, NOT
BECAUSE YOU DON'T CARE, BUT BECAUSE THEY DON'T."
—MELCHOR LIM

CHAPTER 4:
THE POWER OF ANGER

Most of us who go through a big life change will experience anger. Anger is a completely normal and powerful emotion that can sustain us through very hard times or provide resolve to get unstuck.

Anger in and of itself is not a problem – it is what you do with anger that can help or hurt.

Anger can be the catalyst for great change if you express your emotions and assert your needs.

Anger can also slowly eat you alive if you don't let it go when it is safe and healthy to do so. Pain and anger go hand in hand, but for me, anger was the emotion that motivated me to save myself. In self-preservation mode, anger can propel you to remove a person, place or thing from your life to resolve the pain.

For example, in cases of spousal abuse[3], the abused may take the physical and mental pain for an extended period of time believing

---

[3] There are many forms of abuse, all significant—physical, psychological, emotional, financial, spiritual. If you find yourself in this situation, seek help in a support group or a therapist. If you are in danger, call the National Domestic Violence Hotline at 800-799-SAFE (7233).

they are at fault or feeling powerless. Anger in this situation could be the motivating factor in making a decision to leave the situation. Anger is a shield here, motivating someone to protect themselves.

Denial to Blame

When I first learned of the infidelity, I was in denial and badly wanted it to be untrue. Anything but the betrayal had to be true. I began to again feel stuck in the mode of rationalizing the events that had so drastically upended my life.

> Stuck in the pattern of trying to make sense of the burning house rather than get out of the burning house.

In one of our couples therapy sessions about one month after the revelation, my husband admitted that he did not think we should try to reconcile because I would never forgive him. He was wrong about that, but it was true that I would probably never trust him again.

Looking back, I recognize this as a symptom of his deep shame and inability to forgive himself or likely to ever accept my forgiveness could I give it. It was also a reflection of how stuck I was at the time. I was a long way off from forgiving him - more on that in Chapter 5.

My therapist later said to me, "Six years is a long time to be pouring your love into another person outside the marriage. I hate to say it, but he probably can't get back."

Once the panic subsided, the reality sunk in. I had suspected this reality for many years, but was repeatedly made to feel like my suspicions were unfounded.

Now the fog was lifting and I was beginning to transition from denial. Actually accepting this reality now felt scary, but it also gave me a choice. *A choice to get unstuck.*

Tipping Point

Most therapists or counselors agree that if a marriage is going to have a chance to come back from infidelity, the partner with the transgression must not be in contact with the person on the other side of the infidelity. While I was reconciling myself to the realization that we were headed for divorce, it was agreed that contact with the other would cease to give us space to have a clear path forward.

One day, I discovered messages on his phone from the other woman. The shock of seeing their recent conversations gave me resolve and strength. This new emotion - anger - born in resoluteness and strength, ran through me as I read their conversations.

Finally, the denial was melting away and turning into something useful, a motivating, self-preservationist anger. The blame-based narratives fell away and I had clarity. Once I was angry, I was able to contemplate filing for divorce. The next morning a calm came over me and I could see very clearly my next steps. I drove to the lawyer's office, wrote a check and signed the paperwork.

Until I saw those painful messages, I had a shred of hope that kept me from letting go. Of course, it was a long time before I *actually* let go of all the hopes and dreams I'd had for our lives together. But with my new resolve and clarity, I could let him go.

I've read in many places that letting yourself feel the pain is the only way to work through it.

But what does it mean to "feel the pain?" How does one step out of the cycle?

The best explanation I've heard of this concept comes in a book called _The Untethered Soul: The Journey Beyond Yourself_ by Michael A. Singer. He explains that emotions such as pain and anger are energy and each person has to choose how to use their own energy.

"When you feel pain, simply view it as energy. Just start seeing these inner experiences as energy passing through your heart and before the eye of your consciousness. Then relax. Do the opposite of contracting and closing. Relax and release. Relax your heart until you are actually face-to-face with the exact place where it hurts. Stay open and receptive so you can be present right where the tension is. You must be willing to be present right at the place of the tightness and pain, and then relax and go even deeper. This is very deep growth and transformation. But you will not want to do this. You will feel tremendous resistance to doing this, and that's what makes it so powerful. As you relax and feel the resistance, the heart will want to pull away, to close, to protect, and to defend itself. Keep relaxing. Relax your shoulders and relax your heart. Let go and give room for the pain to pass through you. It's just energy. Just see it as energy and let it go."

— **Michael A. Singer, _The Untethered Soul: The Journey Beyond Yourself_**

Freedom

Before filing for divorce, I planned a very long hike in Spain for May and June of 2018. While in Spain, I decided that I would indeed sell my business. I didn't want the company to get caught up as an asset during the divorce. Most importantly, I knew I needed to focus on myself and not bury myself in the day-to-day work.

I mentioned earlier in Chapter 1 that I did sell my business. It happened in October 2018, just months after returning home from the Camino de Santiago. It was the best of both worlds in that I was staying on in a paid position without all the stress of small business ownership.

In 2021, I had fulfilled the commitment of staying three years to run my company for the corporation that purchased it in 2018. Should I choose, Oct. 1 was freedom day.

For three years, I had been dreaming up different scenarios. I would work for a nonprofit in the news industry. I would sell my house, downsize to a condo and buy a second condo on a beach somewhere. I would find a remote sales position so I could travel while I worked.

Only one thing was for sure, I knew I needed to be by the ocean. I had waited my whole life to live by the water and now was my chance.

My kids were all out of the nest, employed, insured and housed. They all had their own lives, their careers and their partners. No grandbabies were in sight. My parents and my in-laws were healthy.

This was my time and I knew I needed to take advantage of this window and create a new life for myself. Even though the money was good and I had every material thing I needed, I was not living a fulfilling life. I was living a version of my old life and it didn't fill my soul any longer. This town in Tennessee was too small for me now.

It was a long process to think through what I wanted but it came down to one word. Freedom.

The Big What If...

In January 2021, I went to meet with my financial advisor, and we worked through several scenarios. One was the downsizing of my house and buying a second home, a beach condo. Another scenario was completely different and as scary as it sounded, it made my heart sing to think of it.

The big what if. What if I sold my house, gave away everything and traveled for one or two years?

What if I completely freed myself of the baggage of my marriage, the furniture, the pots and pans, the photo albums, the lamps, the rugs, the dishes?

Everything had memories.

What if I was completely free to go wherever I wanted and see whatever I could see? Who knows what I may find out about myself? Who knows who I might meet along the way?

Because of my bonus for having stayed three years with the corporation, I had some money set aside for such a dream. By February of 2021, I made the decision to follow through with this plan.

Maybe, just maybe, I would find a way back to a fulfilled and happy soul.

I sold my house in May 2021 and downsized into a one-bedroom apartment on an 8-month lease through December. I gave notice to my employer over the summer and I retired from that industry on Oct. 8.

I began my year of adventure.

The Journey

Throughout my journey over 2021-22, I had a lot of time to reflect on my life since October 2017. Much had happened and I found myself grateful for the path I had literally and figuratively walked.

By May 2022, my travels included the Grand Canyon, Utah, Mexico, Patagonia, Buenes Aires, Portugal, Azores and Spain. Lots of miles were put on my hiking boots and lots of smiles on my face!

At the end of April 2022, I flew home to help my middle daughter and her partner move. My main jobs were to help clean the apartment after moving out and then help her drive her car to their new home state.

After helping complete the move, I flew back home for a May wedding shower for my oldest daughter. We had an amazing time with family and friends. It was a beautiful evening and everyone felt gratitude for the love of this young couple.

I felt like it was important to have our family together, especially our core family of five. I have a divorced friend who said to me in 2021, "We are still a family - it's just a different version of our family."

My wise friend, Kaye, says that your pain does not have to diminish your joy for others. No matter what loss you have suffered, you can still be happy for others. I'm grateful she taught me this through example after the death of her beloved daughter.

Following that celebration, the plan was to drive my car up to New England where I would spend the summer and be available to help with the wedding plans. During the summer, I hoped to find a place to live after my year of travel. It was another exciting adventure ahead of me - my first New England summer.

So many great things were happening, but had I healed?

The Secret and the Truth

On the drive up, I stayed with my dear friend Loretta at a halfway point. I had not seen her since 2020.

Loretta, her partner and I had dinner outside that night, enjoying the late spring chill in the air. I shared my journey of the last eight months with them and updated them on my girls. We talked about the wedding and my future plans.

After we were settled in, we began to discuss the divorce recovery and where I was in the process. Loretta's marriage ended very similarly to mine and it was a painful thing we shared in common. But it was also a blessing to me because she knew from the inside out what I had been through and being ten years ahead of me in the process, what I have yet to face.

Loretta and I spoke late into the night and again the next morning. I could tell she had something on her mind and she had something to say.

Our discussion changed many things for me and, in a way, it propelled my healing forward. I will always be grateful for the love she gave me that day, even though it didn't feel so great at the time.

Loretta Interview Part 1

Let's chat with Loretta shall we? The original conversation referenced above was in May 2022 and our interview below takes place in November 2022. This conversation will be split into two parts, the second found in Chapter 5.

Kelly
OK, so background, Loretta, can you talk about your career, marriage and the kids?

Loretta
I grew up a quiet, insecure little person. I had a lot of learning disabilities. I was a slow learner. They didn't put you into any category back then. You were just the slow learner kid in the corner. My brother and older sister had good grades, no problem. And then there was me.

I don't think I started talking until I was three and a half. And I think probably, auditorily, I couldn't pick it up. My sister is this huge personality and I hid behind her. She is probably the reason why I didn't talk - she learned whatever I needed to say and would talk for me.

I didn't go to college. My parents were divorced at that time. My father had college savings for me, but I didn't want to go because I didn't like girls and groups of girls, right? We moved four times from 8th grade to high school so I knew all about girl groups and how hard that is.

Kelly

Is that where you met Katie [my family member and Loretta's best friend]?

Loretta

Yeah, that's where I met Katie. The girls were very cliquey and those kids had gone through grade school and junior high together, so the cliques were pretty well made.

And I was cute. That's not a good thing to come into school with cliquey girls. It doesn't go well at all. I was a real loner. I just marched to the beat of my own drum.

I didn't want to go to college, probably subconsciously, because school was so hard for me. I went to visit my sister at her college when I was a senior in high school. She was joining a sorority and they sat around in a circle and were doing all this sorority shit, inner circle stuff. And I remember thinking, "This is like a horror extension of high school."

I'll stick to my house and go dig my garden. There's no way in hell I'm gonna go torture myself for another four years. I became a dental assistant after I graduated from high school, and after a year, I decided I wanted to travel. So I traveled out west for a year and a half and just camped along the way with a girlfriend. That was a fantastic experience for me.

I came home only to visit my family for the holidays and that was when my sister introduced me to her boss Willie who was 8 years older. I moved in with him and then I had my 21st birthday somewhere around there.

I got married when I was just 21. Willie is a huge personality so then I hid behind him. It was always about me hiding behind larger personalities and being the quiet person. That was my safe place. I even wore oversized clothes to hide me.

I helped Willie create his dynasty. I worked with him in building his medical practice. I was a people pleaser, wanting to help build his dreams.

I really didn't have any dreams of my own. I wanted to be a stay-at-home mom, but didn't become a mom for a long time. I think we were married for seven years before we had kids because I was busy building.

I'm a hard worker and I don't know where that comes from. My goal was to help him build and work my ass off to do that. Then at age 30, I had my son and at age 33, I had my daughter. I stayed home with the kids then.

Willie is an unusual person. I mean I still love him today. You can't not love Willie - if you don't get mad at him for different things he does. But he's fun. He's an outgoing personality. He's a nice guy. But he's his own human being. I didn't realize this for a while - he doesn't know how to connect with people.

It was really interesting years later. Mac and Willie and Mac's wife Rose all went to college together. We all met up with some other university friends who don't live in the area. We're walking around the school and we're talking and Mac said, "How's Willie doing?"

I said, "Oh, he's good, remarried." [after 2003 divorce]

Then he asks, "How is his relationship with his children?"

And I thought honestly, you know, for somebody I don't really know very well, this is a weird question.

I said, "Willie was the perfect coach dad. He was the coach of every single team for the kids."

Willie was a huge athlete who was a prom king. He was captain of the football team until he cracked his back and then he became captain of the basketball team. He's very talented athletically.

But in relation to anything else, he wasn't around. I always said and everybody said, I was married to an invisible person. I did life as a married person, but really not being married.

He was there for the coaching, but then he would just get involved with other projects. He was always learning and searching and doing things and the kids and I were not part of it.

I went through years of being sad and unhappy about it, crying about it, over and over and over again. And it never got corrected to where I learned to not be sad.

Thank God that's when I got involved with [the company] and started my own career. Thank God I had that because this became my other thing that I could focus on. I started developing myself - so then the project was myself. And so it was me and the kids and [the company].

Then, with Willie, my attitude was, if you'd like to join us, you could join us. That's great. But if not, OK.

We just became roommates. We weren't the arguing types. We just coexisted in the same house for years.

Through that process, I grew and developed myself. That's actually when I realized the rest of the story. You know, I knew he was having an affair subconsciously. My sister even tried telling me.

Willie told my sister he was going to go out to Seattle to this course with his assistant Barbara and invited my sister to join them. Barbara was not really an assistant. She was one of his patients that he had healed dramatically. She became enamored by him.

And so he, Barbara and my sister went out to take the course in Seattle. And when my sister came back she said, "Do you think Willie's cheating?"

At that point, I wasn't denying it. I almost didn't want to hear it. I didn't realize how much of the fog I was living in. I thought depression is only if you're making yourself miserable. I wasn't miserable because I had other things to focus on, my business and my children. OK, I just didn't want to hear it because I didn't want to have to deal with it at the time.

In a way, the next step was too scary. I was unhappy. I was certainly depressed. There were times that I was so depressed, I would dream about Willie dying. And then I would think no, he's too healthy. He's not going to die. I never dreamed about murdering him.

But I dreamed that I could just kill myself. That may be the easiest thing. So I can totally relate to people who kill themselves. I totally understand it because I was that depressed and didn't realize I was walking around carrying it. I wasn't talking to anybody about it.

I guess you could call it denial, whatever you want to call it. I just didn't want to go there. It would mean breaking the family apart. You just move on.

At that point, we were sleeping with a pillow between us because he said his shoulder hurt from an old basketball injury. So he slept with the pillow, lifting it up and there wasn't any sex at that point.

The affair had been going on for seven years. That's when our financial guy contacted me. He was a college buddy of Willie's too.

He said, "Loretta, Willie is starting to pull money out of some of your really big investments."

That was strange. Willie would never touch the money. Willie never did anything. I took care of everything. I buy his underwear. I buy his shoes. He never even went to the store. He never signed a check. He never did anything. He didn't even know what we had.

Willie had called the financial guy and he didn't know the account numbers. So the financial guy knew something's up.

That's when I thought, OK, damn it. I made some phone calls and I realized he was taking the money out because he and Barbara were setting up their own account, supposedly for the alternative medical practice that he has. But that's when I blew the whistle.

I always say, looking back, it was really sad that this was what had to be the whistle. That's how little I thought of myself and how little I believed in myself that I wasn't going to end the marriage because he had another woman. I was going to end the marriage because he was taking the money that we had worked hard together to accumulate and put into our investments. It was the money that did it.

Thank God for immersing myself in personal development. I don't think I would have handled the divorce as well. And I handled it really well. I'm sure there were periods of anger, hatred and sadness that I can't remember. OK, you're always gonna remember the good stuff. I thank God.

Kelly

Like a grieving process.

Loretta

It is. I think rejection is so hard. Mac, who became my new partner, says, "What you went through is so much worse than what I went through with Rose. Rose left this world because she had no control over her illness. You were rejected."

Kelly

When you and I first talked about what happened with my marriage, you said that to me. Rejection. I said, "Don't say that." I was sitting in front of the post office. I know exactly where I was when I called you. I didn't want to hear that. It was painful.

Loretta

No doubt. I know where I was standing too. I was in Cape Coral, Florida at one of my [company] retail clubs [that she owned]. I walked outside the club and had this conversation with you, walking up and down the sidewalk. You know, what's really crazy?

Willie and I were separated for two to three years. So I was shocked at the pace that you moved. I was like, oh my God, I could never move at that pace.

I bought a couple of books and The Secret [by Rhonda Byrne] was the first book I bought online. I don't know why. Well, you know, when God talks to you, He just says, "You go read that book, go look it up."

I ask myself, "Why am I looking at that book?"

I've learned to just buy or just do and listen to Him. And then my sister gave me a book, In the Meantime, about falling in love with yourself. That book was incredible.

Kelly
Is that when you would say you started healing?

Loretta
Yeah, I think so. Understanding the whole process is healing. I mean, our whole life is healing. But those two books were biggies that just helped me. Reading about other people's lives that are far, far worse than ours and the fact that they got through.

It doesn't even matter how they got through it, but the fact that they did. It's that hope at the end of the tunnel. It's just unique.

You know, when Hank [her former boyfriend and a family member of mine] had his accident [in 2008], I could not stop reading books about brain injuries. I probably bought 10 to 15 books and read books about successful brain injury recovery stories.

It's just like that light at the end of the tunnel to keep you moving.

And 2006 is when _The Secret_ came out. It was just another personal development book that came out and I would jump on it. It was well talked about in my circles and Oprah was talking about it. My [company]] sponsor loves Oprah.

So I fell in love with _The Secret_ and I'm trying to get my kids to read The Secret.

My son says, "Jesus Christ, Mom, what the hell, Dad's on us about this damn book and I don't have to hear it from you."

I think I laughed and thought, "Isn't this interesting? We're still going down the same path. We are two spirits that should have been together and for whatever reason, we're not."

What this book gave me is the ability to learn how to, on a daily basis, bring your gratefulness up to the forefront of the day. And then _The Power_ is the next book about words. I learned how to write my gratefulness down every day and my affirmations after that.

Kelly

I think you may have answered this, but then we're going to come back to The Secret, trust me. So, you began to heal before you even got divorced? I mean, you started looking for answers and following the signs. This chapter is about anger, you know, we all have anger.

I've also learned and read in other sources that anger can be a shield and then it can be an anchor. It can be a shield that gets you from point A to point B, but then you've got to put it down. For example, I had to get mad to file for divorce. I was hurt, rejected all of those things. I couldn't go file for divorce. I was too weak.

And once a couple of things happened, my anger was ignited and fueled. And so within 24 hours, I filed for divorce. I mean, it just took that thing - that anger. I felt kind of like Wonder Woman because I took up that shield and just ran to my attorney. Don't let anything stop me.

I think there's also the working through the pain, sitting with the pain and letting go of the pain.

When I saw you in 2020 when I stayed with you on a drive to Boston, we talked about the pain and the rejection and we had very similar stories. I was seeking healing but I was also busy working hard for the people who bought my company.

So here we are in 2021. I do the "great cleansing of 2021" and sell the house, give away all of my things and I start to travel. And I'm traveling, I'm meeting people and I'm feeling so great about my life and the choices I've made. I'm really proud of myself. I went to Portugal and I hiked a Camino and then our friend Dan passes away. I came back in April and I had a tough conversation with my family about boundaries involving my ex.

We talked it out, hugged it out, but it had left me feeling unsettled. I was seeing and hearing my pain in my words. And yet, I thought I'd already worked through all the pain. I didn't think I was angry.

That's where I was mentally when I drove up from Nashville in May of 2022 and stayed the night with you. You and I were having a conversation and you said so many things in that conversation that hit me square between the eyes. But one of the things you said was, "Your pain makes them uncomfortable."

And then you and I went on a walk the next morning. Do you want to tell that story because I think it's more important coming from you about what you saw in me and what you were feeling. Tell me about what you saw?

Loretta
Tell me what you remember hearing me tell you.

Kelly
I think the night before you were definitely sympathetic, empathetic that my family was not able to give me what I needed. You really didn't bring up that you were seeing anger in me.

Loretta

That night.

Kelly

But the next morning you were making me tea and you said, "I'm supposed to give you this book." It was the one about starting in the basement and cleaning all the way up, _In the Meantime_ [Iyanla Vanzant].

Loretta

Did I give it to you? Yeah, my sister gave it to me. Wow. Cool.

Kelly

The next day we went on the walk and you said to me, "You're still angry."

I disagreed but admitted my family was telling me I was angry.

And I was saying, "No, I'm not. It just still hurts. It's not over for me. I'm not angry."

And then you started talking about _The Secret_ and that I had to figure out a way to let it go and be happy for them [my ex and the other woman who was now his partner] and that I, basically, wasn't going to be happy until I could be happy for them. All I had was cuss words coming out. I was thinking "screw you" or "how dare you say that?"

Loretta

That is the secret. You have to realize Kelly, I was very kind with you. Sometimes people don't really want to be mentored by me because as I've grown older, I really tell it like it is. I've lost friends over it but they're not people I should be friends with, right? If I can't tell you what's going on and what's reality, then.... so I was pretty nice with you.

Kelly
I think it's important for people to hear from you. What did you see?

Loretta
What did I see? I saw somebody who had pain. What we don't understand is the pain versus the anger. We get it all mixed up. But it doesn't matter what we call it.

This is what The Secret is to me. _The Secret_ is the law of attraction. I say it's like the Bible. You know with the Bible, we practice a certain rhythm in our life. Those of us who do some sort of Bible reading in the morning or go to church everyday, it is to connect you back to that spiritual place. I'm trying to be non-religious here.

It creates - it sets up - a rhythm for you in your life and in your mind. I'm always mentoring many different people from different religions and people who are different colors. It's hard to do and what you say is it's truly about the physics law, the law of attraction, the law of energy.

The Secret is just teaching us how to practice that. So, your pain, whether we want to call it anger or pain, it is this thing that's in you still.

You've come to a new level and it's going to be really neat to see you ten years from now. Wow. You're going to see, it is just the process. We can't do these things overnight, you know?

But practicing is important and that's why I am listening [on Audible] to The Secret over and over again. I love listening to it instead of reading it. It reminds you of how to practice it because we all, just like a good Christian, we all fall.

Another great book is _Outwitting the Devil_ by Napoleon Hill. It's not about love or anything like that. What was really cool is I've read all these personal development books, for myself and for my business, and then I'm reading The Secret. I went back and read, _Think and Grow Rich_ by Napoleon Hill, for the fifth time and I realize he's talking about the secret. He talked about the secret the whole time in the book, the law of attraction.

We have to get our brain to constantly be thinking of all the grateful things in our head every day. We have to ideally start off our day in gratefulness if we can so that our energy level, the boomerang effect, is coming to us.

When we have this pain and we're constantly talking about the pain, that's negative energy. It's a negative energy that has to leave us. It's like when I said I still love Willie, I love him so much. And I don't know if you can say that about Garth [my ex].

Can you say that yet? No, not yet. You will. I know you will, because you're on your journey. This is just part of the journey and 10 years from now, 15 years from now, you're gonna say, I still love Garth. And you'll understand the whole process of why it happened. And what had happened.

I'm not happy that it happened for me. I'm not happy that it happened for you. It's the worst thing. It was the death of our family, our poor children. Oh my God, our poor children. I felt like such a failure as a mom, you know, at least I did back then.

I don't feel that way now because I'm a really good mom that has been a great example for them. And that's my purpose for personal development, continually growing myself to be that example for them of who they will be when they hit these bumps in the road. And they will. And they'll know when they see me. They will see how I got through it and how I got better and what helped me get better and that's what I'm doing with my son right now. Right?

There's a lot of challenges with my son and he has the rest of his life ahead of him, but it's so neat to be that example. As you grow and develop through all of this, it will be for its purpose.

So to me, I wanted to give you _The Secret_ to tell you about the law of attraction. You needed The Secret because you needed to get that law of attraction going for you, to constantly be practicing the law of attraction and to be getting it up into your energy field. And beyond. And then the pain will go away.

You should constantly be thinking about everything that you're grateful for. You're not grateful for Miranda [the other woman, now partner of Garth], you're not grateful for Garth, what they did. You're not grateful, but there's not as much angst towards them right now. And it will be less and less over the years. My divorce was in 2003 - it's been almost 20 years.

I wanted you to get the bad energy, the bad mojo out of your body. We can't have good things come into us or come into our lives unless the negatives are gone because the negative is a boomerang.

I have another great book for you.

During my struggle with trying to figure out when I should retire or even if I should retire, my mentee sent me this book, _The Complete Works of Florence Shin_. It was from the late 1800s, early 1900s.

It's written in old world proper English. She was an orator. I don't know if that's the right word, but people would come to her and she would speak about this stuff. And I'm thinking this is amazing - you're a woman back then and they weren't allowed to talk this way.

Kelly. You're full of energy. You always have been. But [after the divorce] it wasn't all the right energy. It used to be all positive energy, you know? And then it wasn't.

But you don't know until you practice it. That's why I have to always go back and listen to The Secret every couple months. Because we all get bad at practicing it. That's why it's part of my routine to write my gratefulness and write my affirmations too.

Kelly
You had given it to me probably a decade before and I had tried to read it and I couldn't. But listening to it on Audible was totally different. I made myself listen to the whole thing. I could have skipped through the part about money.

Loretta
That's how it works. Money is just an example that works right?

Kelly
I was just thinking that I don't need that part. I don't want that. But when it got to the relationship part, it gave me the words I needed to get the bad energy out. I forgive you. I release you and I want you to be happy.

I mean after listening to everything else. I said, OK, here goes. Driving through Pennsylvania, I say it for the first time.

"I forgive you. I release you. I want you to be happy."

I just felt a whoosh, a physical release. I was thinking, "Oh, wow. Wow."

And then I say it again and my nose starts getting red. I say it again and I started crying. I say it again and I started to believe it. And it felt like a miracle.

Before, I never could find the words. I never knew how to do it. I was just trying to pull myself up a rope, up the side of a building, to happiness again. But the rope was never going to be long enough because I hadn't let go of the pain. You call it anger or pain that I hadn't let go - the energy from the pain and anger.

Loretta
And bad energy can come out. It's not a positive energy that's coming out of you.

Kelly
And that's what I want people to understand from the very beginning of the book - you have the power to heal. It's right here. It's within you. And it's always been there and always will be but you have to choose to use that power.

That power comes from books and exercise and therapy and prayer and all of those things that feed you and help you heal. But if you don't choose to do these things, you're going to stay right where you are. And that's a place you don't want to be, right?

OK last four questions. What feeds your soul?

Loretta
God.

Kelly
OK, when you have a bad day, how do you self soothe?

Loretta

God

Kelly

Do you want to expand on that? You don't have to. I think it's powerful. I'm just asking you.

Loretta

I have my place, my safe place, my safe haven, my 'workshop'. This is my room [office] and that's where I go. If I have a bad day, I'll put The Secret on. If I'm walking, if my brain is in a bad place, I know I have to listen to The Secret.

And what soothes my soul is - there's nothing more important to me, nobody in the world - God. God is number one and he's my best friend. He's my husband. He's who soothes my soul every morning. When I don't go there in the morning, those are my bad days. I'm going to be soothed. That's if I have a bad day - I'm going to try to talk to Him or listen to Him.

So it's Him. I'm always going back to Him.

Kelly

Question three is: what are you hopeful for?

Loretta

That I can keep peace in my mind every day because I work and strive on that every single day. And that my health and for my children and my family to have that to learn to have peace in their mind and have health.

Kelly

Any last advice for people going through a big change?

Loretta

You got to work on yourself. I'm always going to be advising you to listen to something or read something.

For a lot of people, it is always helpful. For me, to read books about people that had it far worse than I did. It wasn't like I was searching out those books but those were the books that I found that really made a difference. Because you've got to go after that.

Kelly

There's no shortcuts. You got to do the work.

Loretta

You got to go after changing yourself. You know, you're changing your mindset. You can't necessarily say it that way to somebody because they don't want to hear that.

They'll be insulted by it, but…

Kelly

They may be but it's just the truth.

Well, I'm grateful to you for introducing me the second time to The Secret.

Loretta

Sometimes it is better to use Audible. For example, you say with self help books, you get two chapters in and you quit because it doesn't keep your interest. Is that what you're saying?

Kelly

I'm saying there was my life before The Secret and then after. You know, in my 20s and my 30s, I was handed self-help sales books. You know how many books you get handed when you're in sales? I just couldn't read them. It was just a block. I couldn't stay interested. And now, since The Secret, I am a voracious reader.

Loretta

In the beginning, I couldn't read either. I would fall asleep because my brain was so weak. I had to start by listening and started with the cassette tape in the Sony Walkman that was clipped to me when I was running. That's how I listened to books. That's how I "read" books.

And then, years later, I became a reader. So now I still read. I allow myself 15 minutes a day to read in the morning. But then, when I walk, I listen. And now walking takes longer than running!

Kelly

It's hilarious that you think you don't have anything to say! You gave me so many great resources. Thank you Loretta, you are one of my heroes!

Empowerment Practice 4:
Find Your Workshop

Loretta shared with us that she self soothes by going to her 'workshop,' which is the name she has given her safe space. It's actually quite a lovely space in her home. She has a rocking chair in front of her fireplace and the chair faces away from her desk where she sits to get her job done.

She can have a book waiting on her or have her Audible version of *The Secret* ready to listen to. This is where she can focus on her healing and her personal development.

Do you have a safe place where you can workshop an idea? If this term is not familiar to you, I will elaborate.

According to the Collins Dictionary, a **workshop** *is a period of discussion or practical work on a particular subject in which a group of people share their knowledge or experience.*

It can also mean *a seminar or series of meetings for intensive study, work, discussion, etc. in some field.*

As you are reading these chapters, there will be items that spark an interest or an idea that makes you uncomfortable. Pay attention to how you are uncomfortable and those sparks. Both are there to invite you to go deeper where you can find healing and hope.

1. Identify a place that makes you feel safe where you can have privacy to think through ideas. If you don't have that privacy in your home, consider getting a study room at a

library, find a park bench, or seek out a chapel at a church. We all need a peaceful place to ponder our next steps when life is providing us challenges.

Whereas exercise provides an outlet for letting out bad energy and creating new, better energy, what I'm suggesting for your workshop space is to be still. Be still and listen to your heart. Know that you are healing. Be still and follow your instincts.

2. Take the exercises you completed in Chapters 1-3 to your workshop space. Review what you have written in or on your vision board and review your resume. Look back at these items. Are there changes you want to make?

   I review my vision board and my vision statement every month at this stage of life because my life is changing rapidly. There are no rules, this is your vision so make sure your hopes, dreams and joy align with your board and statements.

3. Although workshops are sometimes a group exercise, this workshop is for you to do *"practical work on a particular subject"* as the definition suggests. Tackle your doubts, your insecurities, your anger and anything else that is a block for your good energy. My hope is that in being still and confronting these blocks, you will accelerate your healing.

   Consider investing in one of the resources that has been provided by our interviewees. There is a complete list in the appendix and your workshop is a place to invest your time in reading.

Listen to those subtle hints your body will give you. Like Loretta, follow what your inside voice is telling you.

To forgive is to set a prisoner free and discover that the prisoner was you. —Lewis B. Smedes.

CHAPTER 5:
FORGIVENESS IS POSSIBLE

I think many people have a hard time with the concept of forgiveness. I certainly have.

The challenge in forgiveness is that it isn't cut and dry and that it isn't something that you can do one time and it is over. Frequently the act of forgiveness is more like a daily routine such as taking a shower.

When there has been a betrayal, a loss of friendship, or the end of a relationship, many people, including me, get stuck in a place of pain. Even when you work through the pain and you begin to feel happy, you can be haunted by the circumstance or by the person who caused you the pain.

When I began to get to a place of forgiveness, it just didn't seem to stick. I would begin to feel magnanimous toward my ex-husband, and then the pain would circle back around like an old high school bully. But instead of wanting my lunch money, the bully wanted my happiness.

My friend and minister, Kaye, wrote a sermon on forgiveness, which she shared with me.

She said, "Forgiveness is a starting place, not a stopping place. Sometimes we have to forgive every single day, even many times a day, over and over again, or 70 X 7 as Jesus teaches.[4]"

Back in Chapter 4, Loretta had explained the boomerang effect that pain was causing me. When I allowed the pain caused by the affair of Garth and Miranda to affect my life, it was just going to keep coming back around. Until I could fully forgive the affair, until I could release them, I was going to continue to feel the pain.

Loretta pointed out to me that Garth and Miranda weren't feeling my pain because it was uniquely mine. I wasn't somehow punishing them by holding this pain.

The purpose of this pain and anger had been realized already over the last few years. It had brought me to a place where I accepted the divorce and subsequently gained my freedom.

I could see the time had come for me to embrace the freedom and I was the only one who could abolish my pain through the act of forgiveness.

My experience of trying to forgive over and over again seems to be common among spouses who have been betrayed. This is why I want to share with you as honestly as I can how difficult this

---

[4] "Matthew 18:21-22 **21** Then Peter came to Jesus and asked, "Lord, how many times shall I forgive my brother or sister who sins against me? Up to seven times?"

22 Jesus answered, "I tell you, not seven times, but seventy-seven times."

process was for me. The desired result of relief doesn't come swiftly, but when it does come, it is powerful.

Kaye also shared, _The Art of Forgiving, When You Need to Forgive and Don't Know How_ by Lewis Smedes and his take on the three stages of forgiveness really spoke to me. I will summarize these stages within the context of my own experience. I'm highlighting Smedes' stage in bold so you can recognize it as his definition.

Stage One:
"We discover the humanity of the person who hurt us."

Around 2020, after I began to find joy again, I was very uncomfortable when I was around my ex-husband. I could see and feel the guilt and shame radiating from him.

I believe the main reason it made me uncomfortable was because I began to feel empathy for him. I could see that he was also in pain. I could see that he knew the destruction he had caused within so many hearts of people he loved.

The first time I remember feeling this was at our daughter's engagement party. We were working together to pull off a party during the chaos of pandemic restrictions and I was around him for a long day. At the end of the party, with tears in his eyes, he said to me, "We still make a good team."

I couldn't say anything. I just nodded. I saw his pain. I began to see through a clearer lens, as Smedes suggests. I could see him as more than his betrayal and I could see him as more than the lies.

I think I had previously and subconsciously feared that my forgiveness would mean what he had done was OK.

> But forgiveness doesn't condone behavior, just like apologies don't erase the fact that it happened.

But what I could see now that I couldn't see before was his humanity. He was in pain, bruised by what his actions had done to his family.

I would also learn to follow one friend's advice to try look at him simply as the father of my children. This was powerful because it contributed to making him human again. This was the beginning of the forgiveness but I had a long way to go.

Stage Two: "Surrendering our right to get even."
I don't love admitting this, but early in our breakup, more than anything, I wanted my ex to feel the pain that I felt. I wanted him to suffer and I wanted him to know that he was suffering because of what he had done to us.

The way Smedes explains it, I was reserving the right for vengeance, but I learned that vengeance was certainly not going to give me happiness.

As I walked the Camino path in Spain, I was able to see the peace and joy that came from letting go. Just physically being in a new place and creating a new daily existence for myself, made the necessity for vengeance melt away like snow.

My friend Lindsay from the Camino asked me one day if I could find a way to look at every situation that involves my ex with a loving eye. Could I look at every situation through the lens of love?

Lindsay knew that vengeance was not only unhealthy but could potentially destroy me further. And more importantly to me, to seek vengeance could possibly harm my children and my family further.

It was hard to swallow. There were going to be no repercussions for the acts of betrayal that occurred. What was done was done.

I needed to let the fantasy of vengeance slip through my fingers like water and fall to the Camino path where it would remain forever.

Stage Three: "Revising our feelings."

Smedes says that when we give up our right to get even and we see the offender's humanity, our feelings will change. Where before we felt hate, whether it be passive or aggressive, it can be replaced with forgiveness.

Just like I spoke about with Loretta, it was hard for me to conceive of wishing my ex-husband happiness when I had yet to achieve the much-coveted joy of a loving relationship. How could I possibly want his happiness when mine had yet to be found?

When Loretta re-introduced me to the book *The Secret*, it gave me the words to use in my quest to forgive. I began to use those 12 words as a practice in hopes that not only could it be a true and lasting wish, but that it would bring me the peace and joy allowing me to move on with more finality.

These 12 powerful words. I forgive you. I release you. I want you to be happy.

I was reluctant to wish my ex-husband happiness because it meant he would be happy with the other person who had caused me so much pain.

Although I was reluctant and hesitant at first, once I began to find the benevolent intent behind my words, the more real it became.

In reality, I was also wishing for myself these same things.

It was me who needed to be released.

It was me that needed happiness.

And I held the key to unlock those things for myself.

This was my miracle. I could find a way to forgive, to release and to wish happiness for the two people who had hurt me most in my life.

This was Grace I was receiving. I was taking back my power and shining light into my own life. No matter how much my friends and family loved me, <u>I had to do this</u> for myself.

Forgive yourself

Many people have asked me what was the greatest lesson I learned on the Camino. My answer has always been that I learned to forgive my ex-husband and more importantly, myself. I get some funny looks on the second part of that statement. I see the question in their eyes.

I had always been a strong person and someone that my friends and family could rely on. I was a joyful person and I loved to give. I could also be stubbornly focused on achieving a goal.

But when it came time to protect myself from the person I loved most, I failed. I failed to stand up for myself. I failed to recognize what was right in front of me. I didn't leave when I could see I was unloved. I didn't stay married like I had dreamed.

Writing this book has given more weight to the statement that I had to forgive myself. Just as I continually worked to forgive Garth and Miranda, I continued the work toward my own forgiveness.

So here, I say it again…

Kelly,

I forgive you.
I release you.
I wish you happiness.

You are loved.
You are more than enough.
The best is yet to come.

Loretta Interview Part 2

In this second part of the interview with Loretta, we talk about a shift in mindset in how one can shift a view of the situation. We also talk about the empowerment that comes from taking responsibility.

Loretta

I'd like to share another really good thing. I don't know if I've told you about how this happened in my process of my journey of moving forward.

I was a guest speaker at an event and I was the lower level guest speaker and then the higher level guest speaker was Stephen. He was probably my age but started in the business very, very young. I love when he trains. I love when he speaks. I just love hearing how he chooses his words. I can't get enough of them.

We were on the first part of the three-day meeting and he said, "Listen, I'm going to leave on your last section. I have somebody I need to pick up at the airport, but I'll be back for the party."

I had never met his wife and I knew he had two little boys. I don't know what ages they were at the time but there were two boys, and I know his wife is petite and dark haired.

He walked in with this bombshell and she was like 5'11" and blonde — younger than him. He came walking in and he introduced her to me as his fiancee. A couple of us old timers who have been around for a while are thinking — what's going on? And then somebody said he was divorced. I had no idea.

So the next morning, we sat down to meet again and I said, "Stephen, I just want to say I had no idea you were divorced. I am so sorry."

So obviously, my pain was still raw seven years later for me. I said to him that I knew and understood the pain of divorce and I was so sorry for his loss.

Stephen said, "Thank you. But you know what, Loretta? It's really OK. Everything's really OK. Sometimes what happens in marriages is we change the contracts. The contracts in our marriages get changed."

I was just listening and I had no clue what he was talking about.

He said, "When my wife met me, I was already in [the company]."

Stephen was a Tour de France biker. He was a huge cyclist and he actually went over to France to try to make it — to be one of the best cyclists. He needed money, answered an ad and started selling [the company products] for cash. He then started growing his business all over Europe while he was biking and he ended up being very successful, not being one of the best bikers, but he became very successful with [the company].

When he met his wife, he said to her that his business is [the company] and I travel the world. That's my business. It looked fun to her.

Eventually it came time to have babies. Now, she's got the baby and he's still traveling the world. Right? And then another baby comes and he's not going to end his career. His career is who he is and that means traveling the world. And so she ended up finding somebody who would be willing to stay at home and be a dad to the children and a husband.

Then he said, "She wanted a different contract. She signed up for one contract and then she just wanted another one. So things change sometimes."

I just looked at him, sat back and I said "OK, thanks."

I thought what a beautiful way to explain that your wife had an affair on you.

At that time, I didn't talk about my divorce. I was getting past it. You're always still healing. Always. But from that time, if I were to talk about it, I would talk about how I changed the contract. I wasn't the person that Willie married. Willie has always been Willie. That's never changed. I changed who I was and I was no longer attractive to him.

Kelly
Because you grew.

Loretta
Yes, because I grew, because I had a career, because I became who I was.

The attraction was lost with you guys. That could have happened to some degree. You grew tremendously and that may have not been the contract that he signed up for. And then the other thing that threw a rock, no, a boulder into the contract was Hank's brain injury [Hank was her boyfriend at that time, and Kelly's family member].

Nobody signed up for that. Nobody. That part sucks and I hate to use that word and I hate that it's a negative word. It is what it is. It just happened. The boulder came.

The boulder came but you changed the contract. You totally grew and changed and developed and that may be a bit of it with a mix of everything with your divorce.

We change, things change. I love the fact that your parents have stayed together. You know, I hope our children stay together in their marriages. They may not. Yeah, somebody may change the contract.

We need to be the example for them. Because when that contract gets changed, you can show them the right way and show others the way — like what you're trying to do in the book.

That's what is beautiful. You understand why I love Stephen — the way he talks, the way he teaches. I want to be like that, to be able to express myself. I love sharing that story because it is a nice way of looking at it, of explaining that in the future.

Just say, "You know what? The contract got changed between us. I changed. There was a family tragedy that really messed up the contract for everybody."

Kelly
I do think the stress from Hank's accident had a lot to do with the disconnection that we had. It certainly was something my ex used to make excuses for his behavior. We both felt guilt about how to handle the aftermath of the accident.

Hank's accident was in March of 2008 and we lost the college funds in October of the same year because of the huge drop in the stock market. And we had a senior in high school. I remember saying out loud to a friend in front of him. "I have to do something. I need to go back to work because we lost our college funds."

And then I thought, "I've got to find a way. How do I balance work and help take care of Hank? But I've got to go back to work. There's no reason for me not to be working."

I even said, "I think it would be good for me to have something for myself so that I don't get lost in taking care of Hank."

[In our poor communication,] this got used against me - I wanted something for myself - and [the fact] that I wanted it was like a trigger [for him] and then it was a trigger for me.

Loretta
Well, it was. Again, you changed the contract, Kelly. Take the responsibility. It's always nice instead of blaming to take the responsibility, you changed the contract. Kelly was the perfect little wife, mother. People pleaser.

Yes, that was your position to have taken on Hank. Correct? Kelly, you didn't do it, you changed the contract. So don't worry that he blamed you or he used his excuse. You changed.

And thank God you did! Just like when Hank [Garth's brother and her boyfriend] dumped me. You said, "Loretta, you know this is good. You should be happy." And I wasn't really happy.

So you made the right decision for you.

Kelly
For my family, I felt like I was making the right decision.

Loretta

Yeah, and the children. Yes, not for Hank's family and their desires. The responsible young Garth who's been the perfect son with his wonderful, perfect wife. Of course, the perfect thing is for you to take on Hank. But you didn't. You got busy with a career to help bring the funds back up and to keep you busy.

So you didn't become that caretaker? That's OK. You know, that's OK. And you changed.

Kelly

Yes. And no. There were much deeper reasons why we didn't take on Hank, not just because I went back to work.

Loretta

No, no, exactly

Kelly

But again, the contract was changed by the tragic accident. And then it changed and then it changed and then it changed and it had to keep changing, because we were in a whole new world.

Loretta

You were and you grew and developed and it's just all different. You know, that's why it's really great. In this day and age, not too many people stay home with their children and also have a career.

Kelly

I did have a career before children. Garth and I were on the same level making about the same amount of money when I left work. It wasn't like I was always an at-home mom.

I had ambitions. I had desires to be a boss, a boss lady, as they say now, but we moved so much. It was impossible for me to do that. I did what I could to bring in money. I sold Tupperware. I was a freelance writer. I did everything to feed that part of myself but always made my family my priority. And I don't regret that at all.

But I felt like I needed to get back to work for the money. I also knew in my heart I needed to go back to work for me. So yeah, I guess you can look at it like a change in the contract. But I looked at it like I was taking care of my family.

Loretta
I changed the contract. Not for any particular reason. It just happened. It just changed. Before, I would take care of whatever he was creating, which is what I always did. And that's how we worked and that's how life was and then all of a sudden, "No, I've got this."

And in some ways, he used it against me too in the divorce and it hurt. It hurts, but it will go away. Working on it helps.

Kelly
That's the thing. I really do believe that anger can be the shield or sword that gets you to where you have to be, but it so quickly becomes an anchor. And the anchor emotions will hold you back and hold you down and not let you be free.

I forgive you. I release you. I want you to be happy. 12 words.

I could forgive Garth. I knew I needed to, but I felt like I had to because of my children. I couldn't sit there and hate on him and be mad at him all the time. It just was not OK for my kids.

I had a much harder time forgiving her [the woman involved] because I'd never even met her. How do you forgive somebody that you'd never even met?

When you said that 'you have to want them to be happy.' You weren't saying you want Garth to be happy. You were saying you want <u>them</u> to be happy.

I had to forgive them both. I had to release them both. I think that is the most important part of all of this. As it came full circle for me and I had this revelation in May, I had about six weeks before I was going to see Garth again at a family wedding.

I had a lot of time to think about what had happened inside of me. I tried to be very purposeful to talk to my friends about it so I had accountability. And I made a practice of saying those 12 words. I forgive you. I release you. I want you to be happy.

Maybe not every day but it was a practice.

Loretta
Good mom. Yeah.

Kelly
Then the first day I saw him in New England was when he came over to my family's vacation rental house. I had invited him to come over for dinner and visit with the groom's family. I pulled him aside and we went outside. I think he had no idea what was coming. I think he just thought I was going to talk about something with the wedding.

But I told him about going through that process. And I said it to him.

I said, "I forgive you. I release you and I want you to be happy."

He was emotional and had tears in his eyes. And he said, "Thank you. I am happy."

I said, "Now it's my turn."

Loretta
Yes! It is your turn. He wants you to be happy.

Kelly
Yeah, he does. But two weeks after that, we all knew what was coming. Dan's funeral was coming and I knew I was going to have to meet Miranda. And for my kids, I had to do it right.

Preparing for that — the process of that — was empowering. It was painful but it was empowering. And it was a huge relief to have it over with or be through with it.

I'm grateful our kids still believe in marriage and they do have memories of us being happy together. Thank God for that.

I feel like it's a miracle, my forgiveness, but it's a miracle that you have to put into practice. You're the one who can give yourself the miracle. Some people don't ever come out of it. Some people don't ever let it go. When you can provide this forgiveness, this release, there is this joy. You're wishing someone joy, which is a beautiful thing.

Loretta
It's a miracle.

Kelly
And nobody can give you that. You have to go searching for it, go looking for it. That's the power. The power is in the joy. The power is in compassion. The power is in love.

Empowerment Practice 5: Meditation for Forgiveness

Smedes' outline for the stages of forgiveness provided me a way to outline my process for you. Now I want to offer a meditation for you to use if you need to walk the pathway to forgiveness.

Forgiveness is so hard. It has taken me years. This is what worked for me and it may be a variation of this that works for you. Please explore and add to the meditation if it helps you.

This practice involves seeing the wounds on both parties, not just yours. It's been hard for me to accept that the other party is also injured but it stands to be true.

Breathing is probably the most important part of this practice. Keeping yourself in a relaxed state will help you gain more insight as you walk toward peace.

Hopefully, you found your workshop as Loretta suggested in Chapter 4. This should be a safe place where you can practice your healing. Let's go there now.

1. Take in five deep breaths. Count to five as you inhale and hold it for three seconds. Breathe out through your mouth with your jaw relaxed. Either close your eyes or keep your eyes half open and in a relaxed state.

2. After you have reached a state of relaxation, continue to breathe normally. Consider who you might need to forgive. It is certainly a valid practice to also consider the need to

forgive yourself.

The point of this exercise is release. The most important step is to recognize that everyone is wounded, including the person you need to release.

Concentrate on where you feel the pain in your body when you think of this person. Is it your heart, your abdomen, your arm, your hips, your neck? It may not be pain, but rather a simple sensation or awareness. Breathe into this part of your body. And take a deep breath again.

In your mind's eye, visualize there is a wound on the person you want to forgive in that spot where you feel the pain.

With care, treat this same wounded area on the person you seek to forgive. You slowly roll a bandage over the wound and symbolically cover their sin or betrayal against you.

You are recognizing this person also has wounds within this relationship and you can both heal. If it is yourself you are seeking to forgive, apply the bandage over your body where you feel the pain.

The bandage is symbolic of empathy, release and forgiveness. Breathe deeply.

3. Next, look at the betrayal and the offending party as if through an unfocused lens of a camera. It is hazy and unclear. As you turn the dial, you create a different perspective.

Now this lens is clearly in focus and is seen from the perspective of a disinterested party who does not feel the need for vengeance or payback. This person can only see the humanity in the mistakes that were made during the betrayal.

Can you be this person looking through the lens? Can you look through the lens with an objective view? Can you look at the situation with detachment? Can you begin to see through a new lens of forgiveness? This doesn't have to be complete, total or final — just a start.

4. Next, can you put words to how you feel after seeing their humanity through a new lens and through the healing bandage? Can you maintain a relaxed state in your mind and body?

Can you repeat these words? I forgive you. I release you. I wish you happiness.

And to yourself, say these words.

I release myself from the pain of your betrayal.
I release myself from the need for payback.
I release myself from this sense of un-belonging.

5. Lastly, you're going to state your intention for happiness. You don't have to use my words, but they are there as a guide. Deep down you know what you need and deep down you know what you want.

I seek peace at all times.

I seek joy at all times.

I live in a state of happiness.

I shine my light on others in love.

I bring empathy and kindness to others.

Lay down for 10 to 15 minutes after this exercise. Keep your mind quiet but try to absorb those last statements of intention. If your mind begins to wander, come back to the intention. This is something you can do every day.

CHAPTER 6:
COURAGE AND VULNERABILITY

Ever accidentally stepped on an ant hill? You have no idea you have stepped on the hill and all of a sudden, your feet and legs are on fire. The ants begin to attack simultaneously the second they feel your reaction and you can do nothing but start knocking them off. The sting from the bites is horrendous and lasts for days.

When the trauma of my marital break-up happened, that's what it felt like. It felt as if every inch of me was on fire and no matter what I did, it still hurt like hell. I couldn't eat. I couldn't sleep but didn't want to get out of bed. I could not stop crying. And to go to work, I needed to do all these things — eat, sleep, move and hold back the tears.

Luckily, I was a runner and my instincts eventually took over. I needed to put my earbuds in, crank up the music and move. And within a few weeks of the bad news, I decided to hike the Camino de Santiago.

Courage Redefined

These steps back into reality take courage and courage is now going to be re-defined for you. Courage is going to have a whole new look. Your new courage is not quite like an athlete who crosses the finish line. It's a bit like a boxer fighting in the ring. But there is a path for you to follow.

The type of courage you need now starts with vulnerability. But, I can hear you now — *"WTF? How could I be any more vulnerable?"*

Right after my divorce was final and I had moved into my new home, my friend Renee recommended Brené Brown's *Call to Courage* on Netflix. This is a video where Brown artfully describes how there is no courage without vulnerability.

This video helped me see myself in a whole new light. I'd always thought wearing my heart on my sleeve and allowing my tears to be seen as weakness. And of course, others had stared at my tears or been uncomfortable with my vulnerability.

Brown says courage comes from allowing yourself to be vulnerable, to be open. Wow, I thought. Does this mean I'm actually brave? And should I try that even more?

> Brown says, "Courage is the willingness to show up when you can't control the outcome."

Over the last few years of my marriage, I had felt a hollowness in my soul. I was closing myself off to people, not being as open as I had always been. My instincts were to cover my pain and to work hard to save my marriage.

Brown tells the story of the impetus for her book *Daring Greatly*. In a tough moment in her life when she just wanted to hide, Brown found a speech given by Teddy Roosevelt in 1910. Please take a moment to read these words. Try to identify with the man in the arena. I sure could.

It is not the critic who counts; not the man who points out how the strong man stumbles, or where the doer of deeds could have done them better. The credit belongs to the man who is actually in the arena, whose face is marred by dust and sweat and blood; who strives valiantly; who errs, who comes short again and again, because there is no effort without error and shortcoming; but who does actually strive to do the deeds; who knows great enthusiasms, the great devotions; who spends himself in a worthy cause; who at the best knows in the end the triumph of high achievement, and who at the worst, if he fails, at least fails while daring greatly, so that his place shall never be with those cold and timid souls who neither know victory nor defeat.

Theodore Roosevelt, 1910

Wow.

I'd like to break this down, using some of the phrases that struck me as relevant to our discussions in this book.

... who is actually in the arena: I believe anyone going through grief from loss, depression, anxiety, addiction, marital strife, a big life change, or trapped in a prison of feeling stuck can identify with the man in the arena. You are in a fight for your life.

... who strives valiantly: It takes guts to get out of that bed every day. It takes massive energy to face each day and what it might bring. Taking a shower, brushing your teeth, going to work, shopping for groceries, driving carpool — can all feel so heavy and unwieldy. But you can do it.

... the great devotions: It takes devotion to care for your loved ones, children or parents during times of difficulty. And you must also have devotion to yourself. Just taking one day — or one minute — at a time is an achievement.

... who comes short again and again: You are going to fail sometimes. You are going to have a bad day. You are going to spiral into the spins of depression on occasion. You are going through a massive life change and these things are to be expected. But these times are always — and I mean *always* — temporary.

... if he fails, at least {he} fails while daring greatly: You must dare to put yourself out in the world again. You must learn to take baby steps, then eventually walk in stride toward your new life. When you begin to date again, when you look for a new job, when you sell your home and move — these are all life choices that make you vulnerable. This is when you know you are daring greatly.

... It is not the critic who counts: Not everyone is going to be on your side or in your corner. There are people who don't want you to move on or feel better. And there will definitely be people who are not going to be happy for you when you move on. *These are not your people.*

Brown says, "You should accept criticism only from people who love you enough that when they see your imperfections, they love you because of them, not in spite of them."

Brown also shares, "Vulnerability is the path back to each other and we can't be afraid to get on it. We want it so bad, but we are so afraid to be seen. And we are afraid to be seen; but it is the only way back."

I Can and I Will

I hope you will take time to watch Brené Brown's *Call to Courage* on Netflix. It has changed a lot of people's minds about vulnerability, and it also gives a great deal of insight into shame and guilt.

After watching the video, even though I was alone in my house, I began to say aloud things I had felt while watching. Brown's words lit a spark in me. I instantly recognized some non-negotiables deep within my soul and I said them out loud. The sound of my voice was convincing and it felt good to fill the room with the sound of my hope.

I will not close myself off from the possibility of love.
I will not close myself off to moving on.
I will not be afraid to find out what the "new me" is going to do in my life.
And I will not stop believing in love.

Then, I realized these were spoken in a negative frame of mind, almost like I was giving myself new limitations, when using the words "I will not." So, I started over with "I can" and began lifting myself up with statements of belief in myself.

I can get up and go for a walk every day and I'll bring a friend if I need the support.
I can begin to look at job listings to find out what interests me.
I can listen to music that builds me up.
I can start a list of what I like about myself.
I can begin to look in the mirror every day and say I love you to myself.
I can go buy myself a new dress, negligee or underwear — something that makes me feel pretty.
I can see that all of my accomplishments still matter.

I can feel I'm loved and admired by my children.
I can believe I will be loved deeply again someday.

I can, I can, I can and I will.

Crystal Interview Part 1

I want to share with you a unique perspective from my friend Crystal. I'll ask her to give you her amazing background and transformation story. Then she will share about a time in her life when she was completely vulnerable and what steps she took to understand her next steps.

Kelly
Please give me your background.

Crystal
I grew up in Tennessee and have lived there all my life. My father was a Methodist minister.

I met James in college. We got married right out of college and four years later I had my first son. And 18 months later I had my second son and 18 months later had my third and two years later, had my fourth. From then on, I was pretty much a mom.

I wanted to raise my kids in the church, right? So I have kids and go back to church and I looked into bible studies. I wanted an academic Bible study because they asked different questions. They asked big picture kinds of questions. I started taking Disciple Bible Study and I loved it and the study began to give my life a framework for everything I thought about religion and spirituality.

I participated in this study for three years. During the summer after my third year of study, while on vacation, I had a voicemail from the adult discipleship leader at church.

I thought, "Oh, no, she's gonna ask me to teach."

I knew it, so I didn't answer her calls. She kept calling me and eventually I agreed. I'm so happy I said yes.

I loved teaching. I loved learning with my little flock. They were like my little sheep. I loved taking care of them. Praying for them. You know, I loved watching them grow.

I love that we asked those hard questions. And I love that we were trying to do this and also living in that world in [a wealthy community].

We were soccer moms, volleyball moms, church volunteers, PTO board members, and we were exhausted.

We believed that's how we're supposed to live life. I remember one time, Kelly, you asking me, how are we supposed to live like this? I'm so stressed out by the time I come to church because my Sundays are so full with all the obligations my family has for church. This does not seem right to me. We just talked about it and faced it and were honest about it.

After teaching bible study for three years, our church began a new contemplative service on Wednesday nights called The Well. I went to the pastor's office one day to say Wednesday is my church day and I would love to be a part of The Well. That's why I went into her office.

But when I walked into her office, and for the first time ever, I noticed her bookshelves. I had not noticed the bookshelves before. I remember as I stood there staring, an individual book would jump out and then I would look over here and this other book would come into focus.

So instead, what I said to her was, "I want to read all those books."

She said, 'Oh, just go to divinity school.'

"What is Divinity School?" I asked.

And she asked, "Is this really what you came here to talk to me about?"

And I said, "Yes, I want to know. What would this look like? How would I do this?"

Kelly
Do you know what year that was?

Crystal
Probably 2006. She said to go down to the school and hang out, walk around, you know, check it out. So I did.

I loved it every time I did it. I would just go to the library and open a book. I began to think, what if this was my job? What if this is what I'm supposed to do every day, read and think and have conversations that matter?

And for a couple of years, it was all just a big 'what if' — then one snowy day, it must have been January 2008, this little nagging voice was in my head going, "You know, this is the deadline to apply for Divinity School. I had two essays to write."

And I was like, "Are you serious? I have a house full of boys and wet clothes and they're starving and they're eating everything in the house? This is the day you want me to fill out this application?"

So I sat down and typed up the applications and wrote the essays.

In my mind, I'm thinking a lot has to happen for me to do this. I need this much money. I need to know that I cannot be expected to complete this in three years. I will not go during the summer. And I will not take more than three classes each semester. I just said those things in my head.

When I got the acceptance letter back, it was exactly in that order.

Here's your scholarship aid. You have seven years to complete your degree, as long as you remain a full-time student in the fall and spring semester and that's three classes. It was every single thing that I had worried over. And then I just was like, "God, you're such a show off!"

I began grad school at age 42 in the fall of 2008. All was going well until the summer of 2010. And then I found out that James is having an affair with this woman from his high school. I was completely destroyed, crawling up in the fetal position in my closet.

One friend came to sit outside my door. I was afraid I might not come out. She would sit outside to keep James away from me and set a timer to say, "It's been 30 minutes, are you OK?"

I fought for my marriage and we did a lot of work. When James and I were working through all this, I was thinking I might have to drop out of grad school.

In marriage therapy they ask, "What are you giving your energy to that you should be putting into your marriage?"

I thought maybe it's grad school. And maybe I don't need to do this because I need to put my energy back into marriage.

We had a female Associate Dean, so I made an appointment to talk to her. But when I got there, she couldn't meet with me and I had to meet with another advisor and he's a guy about our age.

He turned out to be the right person to talk about it because he said he had cheated on his wife.

Wow. I mean, I just had my first lesson in being vulnerable. I just show up like other people.

I had believed he was standoffish in a way.

He went on to say, "I've been where you are but I was the cheater."

And he said everything was going wrong at home, that he was getting so much praise and so much positive reinforcement in his career.

He said, "I chose my career."

So I thought that he was basically telling me, OK, yeah, you're right.

He wasn't.

He said, "I appreciate that you would give this up for your marriage because I wasn't willing to do that. But, I'm not sure it's the right path for you.

> And I have one question I want to ask you,
> "What do you feel?"

Nobody ever asked me that. And immediately I said, I want to be a learner. I've been a teacher. Now I want to be a learner. I think it's so important for me to be in community with people much different than home.

I told him I didn't think I could continue full time and that was a problem because if I dropped below three classes, I had to pay full price. And it wasn't possible for me.

For that moment, he was able to be present with me. I stuck it out. I'm so glad that I did. I started writing in my classes from this new place.

I started writing from this place of vulnerability because of something he said.

"You think you're doing this for God? This school is God's gift to you — make it what you need it to be."

I said to him, "I'm halfway through, but I don't want to be ordained clergy. I don't want to take specific religion courses. I've already lived that life."

Some other mothers went back to work and some started golf and tennis. As for me, I went to divinity school. I said I didn't know what I would do with it.

And then he was so human.

He said, "You are the luckiest student. This [school] is God's gift to you. So you study where your heart is leading you to study and you make this work for you. And you will graduate. It looks worse on us if you don't graduate than it does on you. We have more at stake in this than you do."

It totally flipped my perspective of not being able to graduate. And, wow, it really has turned out that way. I had taken it for granted because it was the only seminary close by me.

I made it through and finished. Those last three years were hard.

During those difficult times, I started going up to the mountain in Sewanee, Tenn every two weeks. I would go and I would cry while I sat with Jesus in the chapel. I talked to Mary and I would cry.

My kids knew that I was going to the mountain and so they would say, "Will you pray about this for me?"

My friends started knowing about it and asking the same, sharing their prayer requests. It was like me taking care of myself helped other people. Just following my instincts and what my soul needed helped other people's souls.

One day, our covenant group of five women went to the mountain, a holy day together. The next night I got the infamous text from James. Three years later [after his first indiscretion], he was in Tampa fishing and he sent me a text meant for another woman, saying all the things that they were going to do together that weekend. So gross. So gross.

I was just done. So that was five weeks after I graduated from [grad school], my oldest son graduated from college and my third son graduated from high school. I filed for divorce.

Kelly
Thank you for sharing all that. What are some mistakes you made after the divorce?

Crystal
I wanted to learn every single lesson there was to be learned from this because I didn't want to do it again. And that helped me forgive myself when I made mistakes.

There is a quote and I don't know who said it, but it's something like "never waste a good crisis."
And that became my motto.

I had really, really good boundaries with guys. I chose guys who were unavailable romantically, but were good friends, so I had companionship.

I never spent the night over with anybody or let anybody spend the night over with me. I did have really strong boundaries around that. I didn't know if 'just sex' was a thing.

I thought, "Is that possible that it's just sex?"

Kelly
What are some of the things you did right? I think that sounds like that was right.

Crystal
At the same time, I wanted to do this crisis perfectly. I didn't want to make a mistake. I didn't want to be a stereotype. I didn't want to be bitter or be a victim.

I also didn't want to be infamous or notorious.

I said, "OK, I'm not gonna lose 100 pounds and start dressing sexy."

I said to friends, "I don't want a man. I'm not on the prowl. I'm a mess. Look at me. I'm not looking for anybody to save me."

James was spreading rumors about me to get the attention off of him and to make me look like the bad or crazy one.

It was hard because I lost some friends — people I thought were my friends.

But then other people showed up for me and I was so surprised. I had two friends who told me in 2010 they believed I should stay with James to help him find Jesus. I dreaded calling them and telling them about the divorce. Here is the surprise.

Both of these ladies said, "You tried, oh my God. You tried!"

When I told them I was done and I had filed for divorce, I thought that may be a deal breaker for them.

Oh, no. I was wrong.

Instead I heard, "What do you need? We're on your side."

One of those ladies came over the day James and I walked through the house so James could mark which things he wanted. And when he was being a huge asshole, she was there.

She sat there and kept saying, "I'm staying here with you."

I'm following him and she was with us. He was kissing up to her because he thought he had her on his side.

There were surprises, who was supportive and who wasn't.

Kelly
Can we talk about perspective and vulnerability? You shared with me a story about when you had to change how you saw yourself and those friends' perspectives helped you.

Crystal
We were talking about what you wrote, how you felt ashamed, felt alone and felt almost untouchable and unlovable. I felt like that too, but in a different way.

Early in the divorce process, it was really bad what was happening and there's no triage — nobody is worried about me. I kept thinking that I needed somebody to be afraid with me. Why are they not wringing their hands and wondering what I'm going to do?

Nobody. Nobody was worried.

So I was thinking, OK, this is not working. It's not that these people are uncaring, right? I get that. It's not like they don't care.

Did they know something I didn't know? What did they know?

All I could see was everything I didn't have and how bad it could go. I felt like my kids and I were dangling off the cliff.

Also, because of his gambling addiction, I didn't know what would happen if he couldn't pay his debts. I also didn't know about the IRS — there were seven years of falsified tax returns.

And there were the women. I didn't know what kind of crazy women he had out there. What if there's some kind of jilted lover?

I had all those thoughts going on and I already felt unsafe.

I felt so close to all that bad energy and bad people. But nobody else is quite worried about that.

So then I began to talk to you and you said, "You're gonna be fine. What's the worst that can happen?"

I could picture the worst. I said, "I am broke and I'm living in a box on Broadway."

Then you said, "But you'd be free. Would you rather live in this house, in this community with James or live in a box on Broadway with a "will work for $" sign?"

I said without losing a beat, "I would rather live in a box. OK. That box? I can make that work for me."

The worst that could happen to me was that I would stay with James and be forced to live this lie. What if I accepted this weirdo bizarre lie that he kept telling over and over? What if I took a bite of that and swallowed it?

I knew immediately my soul would start to die. This was a gift.

God. Grace. Universe.

When push came to shove in my soul, I didn't care what happened to my body.

I knew my old life was soul killing. Living in a box on Broadway maybe was just a little bit dangerous to me physically.

It was an easy choice to make.

And with that shift in perspective, I could see it because you
and my other friends could see the horizon
that I couldn't see yet.

Because I trusted them, and they took time to love me, I believed that it was out there. Honest to God.

Kelly
You were vulnerable and you trusted them. You trusted their vision of you.

Crystal
Yes, I trusted them. I trusted what they saw — that I was OK.

That was really all I needed to know. I didn't need any kind of specifics. I wanted specifics, but I knew I wasn't going to get them. And so that was huge.

That was a really big stepping stone. Your 'right now.' This is your place — to stay here until the next thing comes into focus.

Step out there and if it doesn't feel right and you think you made the wrong choice, turn around. Go back.

No harm, no foul. You have nothing to lose.

It was a really, really free space to be — It really can't get worse.

I had nothing to lose and so anything I did was to be **unstuck**. But staying on that stepping stone paralyzed in fear was not an option.

Empowerment Practice 6: Recognize Your Courage

"Courage is the willingness to show up when you can't control the outcome," shares Brown in her Netflix special.

Crystal shared with us how she made herself vulnerable with her advisor and with her friends. In doing so, she was able to see her immediate next steps. That was all she needed for this place and time.

After you watch the video, write down 10 ways you can be courageous through vulnerability. Think through who you want to be in the near future — not who you have been.

What actions can you take that propel you into the future?

For example, here are some prompts:

1. I can show up and be seen by…
2. I can ask for what I need by…
3. I can talk about how I'm feeling with…
4. I can have a hard conversation with…

Keep the list going and see all the ways you can show up for yourself.

Then, take it one step further.

Pick one that you will follow through with this week. Pick another that you will follow through two weeks from now.

I encourage you to put a date by each courageous and vulnerable action.

"Out of your vulnerabilities will come your strength." — *Sigmund Freud*

"THE REAL ART OF CONVERSATION IS NOT ONLY TO SAY THE RIGHT THING AT THE RIGHT PLACE BUT TO LEAVE UNSAID THE WRONG THING AT THE TEMPTING MOMENT." — DOROTHY NEVILL

CHAPTER 7:
WHAT I DON'T WANT TO HEAR

Let's get this out of the way… NO person has ever been or will ever be in your situation.

This is an intensely personal moment/day/week/year. Your life, your feelings and your past are uniquely your own. Only you know what is actually going on inside your head and heart.

Therefore I will repeat — you have the power to heal yourself.

When you have had a significant event in your life, people often don't know what to say to you. We all know that empty feeling of wanting to comfort someone who lost a loved one and we believe no words can possibly comfort them. Actually, much healing can come from words in a time of need, as well as a tender touch, a hug, holding a hand, or just simply sitting with someone in silence.

What I want to suggest here is to keep in mind that people do mean well. But in all honesty, the following are words, phrases and sentences that were triggers for anger or frustration for me early on in the divorce. Later, when I was ready to receive them, my feelings were different, of course. You can't control what people will say or do, but you can prepare your own heart to handle such times.

Here come those trigger words.

Relax
It will all be OK
Calm down
Someday you will be grateful
Time heals
It all works out in the end
You need to work on yourself
You deserve better
He doesn't deserve you
They deserve each other
You shouldn't date until you love yourself more
I always thought you guys were the perfect couple
You need to get yourself back out there right away
Everything happens for a reason

People mean well... mostly.

I find it most helpful to have conversations with and to hear from those who have been in similar situations. When these peers say the above phrases to me, I'm more willing to listen and entertain a conversation because it triggers something in me that I need to process. This is the main reason support groups are helpful to some people.

My friend Anna shared with me that she only wanted to talk to widows after she lost her husband. In her mind, no one could understand her grief but them. She was able to find several women who supported her, but not everyone is so lucky.

I have greater hindsight now, of course, to see that the time that was invested in me by others was cause to be grateful. Maybe you can do better than I did and you will be able to receive the gift of their time as it happens.

When people open up to you and share their story, take the time to listen. Don't feel the need to jump in with your own pain. Listen. And hopefully your friends will do the same.

You will come across some people who believe they know how you are feeling and how you should be acting when they have never been in your situation. It doesn't mean they have not felt pain or had trouble in their life. But those who have not been divorced or widowed or suffered a significant loss just don't know how it feels.

On the other hand, a friend or family member who knows your heart and cares for you deeply can still be a sounding board. They can remind you that you are strong, you can thrive again and that they are with you every step of the way.

Consider it a gift when people give you their time, but know that you don't always have to accept their intended gift. Your heart or soul may not be ready to hear what they are saying. Or they may be missing the mark with their interpretation of the situation.

Just be gracious. Be kind. And believe they do want to help. And it's OK to ponder their words and then discard what isn't helpful. Receive and absorb only what helps heal you.

Lastly, you have every right to set boundaries or share your feelings if people are repeatedly attempting to comfort in a way that hurts.

Here are a few things I did need to hear and this is what helped me.

It's OK to be mad.
It's OK to be hurt.
It's OK to feel all these things, just don't let the feelings control you.
You get to create a new vision for your life.

Dating can help build your self esteem if you don't get too caught up in it. This is not the end of your story. I am here for you even if just to listen. YOU ARE ENOUGH!

You must build a plan, a new plan, for your life.

You can start today. You can start tomorrow. You can start next year. But you will eventually have to make decisions about next steps and those will lead to your new life.

For some, the next step may be a plan to get away for a few days. For some, it may be as simple as a trip to the grocery store. Depending on where you are in your journey, just know that it is life-giving to reach toward the future.

How are you doing this in your life now?

I was very lucky to have both divorced and married friends who listened to my relentless self-abuse and soul-sucking loss of confidence. And they also shared their own pain watching my husband and me go through this. They never stopped loving me or supporting me.

What these friends gave me was permission to feel the pain. If you don't work through the pain, it has a hold on you. Working through it means feeling it, sitting with it and allowing yourself time to prepare for the next steps. If you push it down deep inside and throw a smile on your face just to show the world you are OK — you won't heal.

The Getaway Gift

My two friends, Kayce and Shania, rallied around me when they heard the news of our split. As the facts unfolded, they became determined to get me away from my hometown for a few days. It was December and my birthday was coming up so they decided we should go south to Miami.

We quickly acted on the decision using credit card points and airline miles to buy plane tickets and book hotels. Having something to look forward to completely lifted my spirits and I felt almost human again.

On that trip, the three of us laid on beach lounge chairs and ordered lunch and cocktails. We didn't need to move or go and do anything at all. We just needed to be together.

While soaking up the sun, we discussed the options for moving forward in my life, but we also discussed their lives. We talked more openly than we ever had about relationships, motherhood and sex. Lots of talk about sex.

"Why haven't we opened up to each other this fully before?" we all wondered. There was no answer to that, but we were all grateful that we had. We laughed until we cried so many times and the weight began to lift off of me.

One of the servers, Adrienne, came up to us after we had ordered our first round of drinks. She asked if we were there to celebrate something. I flippantly remarked we were celebrating my birthday and my future divorce.

She looked at me with sadness in her eyes and said, "I've been there and it was horrible. But it gets better and he and I are friends now. Baby, you are going to be OK, especially with friends like this."

Adrienne took tender care of Kayce, Shania and me the rest of the weekend. When I went up the last day to pay my final bill,

Adrienne gave me her phone number and said to call if I needed anything.

As I began to walk away, she called me back over to the hut. She shared that she meditated every morning and lifted peoples' names up every day. Adrienne promised to have me on her list for 30 straight days and I should look for that energy.

I couldn't believe that Adrienne, basically a stranger, was being so kind to me and was showing me more love than I had seen in the last six years of my marriage. I cried all the way back to my room — tears of gratitude. The healing continues.

Allison Interview

In April 2022, I hiked my second Camino de Santiago, the Coastal Portuguese route. I met three amazing women on this trek and have hundreds of memories of support, love and kindness.

Two memories, in particular, were with my friend Alison. We discuss them in her interview below, which was in October 2022.

Kelly
Tell me about yourself.

Alison
I am a 56-year-old woman. And I've been a yogi [practitioner of yoga] since I was in my late 20s. Yoga teacher, student. It's my whole life actually.

And through that, I lived a life of being married for 12 years and a mother of a son, almost 22 years now. I was divorced in 2011, I believe that's 12 years ago. So separated and apart, separated longer than 12 years, but divorced almost 12 years.

Kelly
And you are from Canada and are a Canadian American.

Alison
Yes, Canadian American.

I had the experience of divorce in my childhood, which was quite a riveting, shocking experience. And traumatic actually. It was a trauma that I carried with me for many years. And part of my self discovery, self regulation was — I always knew, even as a young child, that I'd have to do some personal work around it.

But I didn't know what that would look like. So that process started in my teens somewhere, wanting to fix it some way and actually wanting to come to terms with the bigness of what transpired for me, within my family, and for my family and all the things that rolled out from that.

So there has always been a self-investigation of some sort. And the one book that I really remember reading, as a teenager, was, <u>How To Be Your Own Best Friend</u> [by Mildred Newman Bernard Berkowitz].

I have another vision of myself standing at my back window and having neighborhood friends come over and ask me questions. Do you remember Charlie Brown and how they had that psychiatry stand? And she was a psychologist or something like that. I think Lucy was sitting at the stand and kids were asking questions and it was kind of like that.

Kelly
It was Lucy!

Alison
It wasn't planned out. It just kind of happened like that. They would say it was kind of funny.

Kelly
I can relate from our Camino. So did yoga become a source of healing exercise? I mean, was it what attracted you to yoga?

Alison
It was always a sense of healing because I had a profound

experience. I was always drawn to it — always drawn to the self and betterment.

When I was 28, I had a "breaking open," which at that time felt like a break down — like a nervous breakdown. I found myself unable to function and manage anything really.

I was completely sitting on the floor and trying to figure out how to fold my laundry. I had been working in a corporate environment and doing all the fun things that 28 year olds do — drink and smoke and party and hang out with friends.

Also I had this large responsibility in a management position and I couldn't seem to do both. It wasn't working for me. And one of them came crashing down and that was my job.

But in the meantime, also, my self nourishment and all my sense of self also came crashing down. So I found myself on the floor trying to figure out how to fold my laundry and moving my body in a way that I hadn't really done in many years since I was in university.

And I thought, "Well, I haven't even really stretched my body hardly ever in the last couple of years."

I could see that I was completely out of balance, obviously. And I had the recognition from 10 years previously, how to "be your own best friend," how to do things to make yourself feel more balanced.

I had done some exercise training and fitness training and I'd studied recreation and all these pieces. I knew that yoga was something that could be really good for my body, mind and spirit, collectively.

Kelly

So you are folding laundry and stretching reminded you. It just kind of brought that feeling.

Alison

Yeah, that integration was really important. It wasn't just one piece. I just always knew that I needed to be balanced — that life was about being balanced.

So I was seeking that out. And I found a spot to go to yoga classes, but it didn't have the right feeling for me. I didn't attend more than one.

And then a month later, I came across a new yoga studio that was opening up. And I said, "I'm gonna check that out."

It was one of those moments in life where I really felt like an absolute, "Yes, go this way."

And I did and I never looked back. I went to the studio and met the owner. And within the month, I started taking classes there and working for her and finding myself changing. I already started changing my life a couple of months previous to that because I knew I had to do something different for balance.

I just stepped into this space. Now I was vegetarian and I was not smoking or drinking and I was sleeping and eating better and nourishing and loving myself.

Kelly

That's amazing. Very cool. That's new info for me. I love it. Thank you for the background. And how old were you when you got married?

Alison

32.

Kelly

I was 21. So it's interesting, I didn't have that job, the one that felt like my nourishing kind of career and I was stepping into myself until I was in my 40s. I did have fun jobs when I was younger and I did work, but it's like life goes for other people.

I'd like to talk about the Camino a little bit. That's where we had our interactions.

Why did you choose the Camino?

Alison

Can you choose? Yeah, well, through that time when I was going through that whole self-discovery process, when I was 28, I read a book called The Pilgrimage [by Paulo Coehlo]. And it was part of my opening.

And there was something in there about "we're all walking each other home." But there was something about life is a journey, it's an adventure, it's… we don't know what's around the corner, one foot in front of the other.

I feel like I've always been a deeply spiritual person and have always felt a calling to connect to spirit. We call it spirit, God, creator, source, whatever term we want to use. I always felt that deeply inside and a longing for that.

And The Pilgrimage, this beautiful book that I read, inspired me to want to live like that. And to actually walk the Camino. It was just a little thing that I had planned in the back of my head, that one day I would do that.

Then I met lots of people that had attempted it and had succeeded doing it and all the different stories, and the desire was still there. But I felt like over the course of time, I heard less about it being a spiritual experience and more about something to just check off of another Bucket List.

And it never was that for me.

So the last few years, we've had this global pandemic, and everything has been turned upside down. Things have really changed.

When there was an opening, I just felt like, "I need to do it now. I don't know why, but I need to do it now."

My draw was mostly walking through Portugal. I don't know why I'm drawn to Portugal, but I'm just very drawn. So that's the way I wanted to go, but I wanted to end up in Santiago.

That's how that came to be. And it really was a lifelong kind of seed that in a moment sprouted. And I said now's the time. I'm going,

Kelly
Yeah, like 25 years later. Wow.

What is a good piece of advice that you received from someone, anyone that made a difference in your life when you were going through a big change?

Alison
There are many, many, many, but the one that I really recall again and again and again,

> ...my best friend said to me,
> "This is going to look different in a year."

Then she would even whittle it down to "this will look different next week."

It actually put things more in perspective. When I felt really stuck and entangled and "this is what it's going to be forever" feeling, I knew that it's not going to last, it's temporary and that it will shift and that if I just don't focus on my belief that it's permanent, then I can recognize that it is temporary and just relax into the knowing that it's gonna change.

Kelly
That's pretty similar to what you asked me that day. You were leading me in a totally different way and I want to talk about that.

Do you remember clearly what you said when we were in the room? You were leading me down the path to think differently about my past or how it would feel. Could I get to a place where I felt differently about it?

Alison
I seem to recall, it was something along the lines of, "Have you considered the possibility of that?" Because we had talked about the fact that [your ex-husband's relationship with] Miranda was a substantial relationship?

It was obviously substance, she was a substantial person in his life, because they had been together at this point for 12 years. And the realization of that — it wasn't a fling, it was another substantial person. And the consideration that this doesn't take away from your value in his life. That was one part of it.

Because you're obviously a very substantial person in his life. And then the second part, "Have you considered the possibility that he went into a relationship with her because you needed to go out into your life and do something else?"

And it wasn't about him leaving you, but setting you free, even if it was unconscious.

Kelly
You are presenting it to me in a way that even in that moment, I didn't get it. It was a couple of months later, when I was listening to The Secret [by Rhonda Byrne], and the writer was saying that if we're feeling pain, it is because we're manifesting pain, or we're holding on to pain from something in the past.

And as long as you're hanging on to that pain, you're gonna keep feeling it. I kept saying I've let it go. I kept saying and I kept believing that I had let it go. And maybe I did. But then I kept pulling it back.

That theme of rejection. I've really been working on that.

When you gave that advice, was it coming from a place that somebody had said it to you? Or had shown you that lesson?

Or was it just something, in the moment, that you saw in me that made you share it?

Alison
I feel like that it wasn't something that someone had said to me, but it was a realization that I had about my own life. I guess it was with my marriage, maybe. But it showed up later, a few years later in another relationship.

And the recognition that life is happening for me, not to me, and that I'm the starring attraction in my life.

How do I want myself to be even in those moments of terror and tragedy and devastation?

We still are totally free to choose how we want to be and how we want to show up and how we respond. I feel like some of that knowledge came along the path of the yogic teachings that I've received over the past three decades and also through the realization and the experience that comes by being immersed in those teachings.

For me, that's been my pathway. And what I heard you say is that you've received it through walking the Camino, you've received it through being inquisitive and curious in relationships with other people as well as through the program that you said you were in [Calling in "The One"] during the summer, and reading some books that were beneficial to you. That helped to flesh out some of those pieces.

It's really the same mountain. It's just different pathways. And the pinnacle at the top of the mountain is the recognition that we are free, and we've always been free and we will always be free.

Kelly
Some really interesting thoughts went through my head when I pictured free, free to go and do, free to think through the love for you, to have or have not, free to be, free to not be. You know, it's funny, you said free and in my mind all these little clouds popped up. Free. Yeah.

Alison
The reason free comes to me is that regardless of what's happening in life, whatever the effects are, they are external, I'm free. I'm not affected by all of those things. I can choose to be at the effect, but I actually am free to not be.

And that my truest nature is not really at the effect of all those things. And that true nature that I'm pointing to is really that nature that we all have. This is that God nature, that Christ nature. It's divinity, divine nature, that's eternal itself.

Kelly

I think one of the hardest things, for some people, about reading something like The Secret or discussing the Divine Self is that in some religions, or if you grow up in America, in a church, you're not taught that you're divine.

I really wasn't introduced to that until the last five years. Even from my friend, Crystal, who's a minister. I didn't hear people talking about, "You are divine because you are made in God's image."

Why would God make you any less if you are made in His image? Right. Of course you are divine because you're His or Hers.

Alison
Exactly right.

Kelly
What did you learn about yourself through the process of divorce?

Alison
One of the most profound lessons that I learned was that in the past I had this belief about myself that I wasn't good enough. And I chose the perfect weather pattern and storm and partner and container and life to reflect that for me so that I could learn that lesson. That was my belief and then also I had to unpack it so that I could be free of that belief.

Kelly
Yeah. Wow.

Alison

I would see it everywhere and it would show up everywhere. But the closest relationship was the one that really highlighted it for me so dramatically that I couldn't <u>not</u> see it and couldn't not attend to it.

Because I'm a self-curious person, I stayed with it. You know, I did. I constantly do the work. And I know not everybody is like that, but I'm grateful that I am. Because it encourages me to just keep expanding.

Kelly

I felt like I kept along those same lines.

I was doing Bible studies and I was doing everything I could to learn to be a good person without ever addressing my own stuff. I think something's going to come out of that. I don't know how this all ends up in the book or what that looks like, but I think that so many women do this. We grow up doing exactly what we were told we should do. We want to be a good person. Do all the right things.

Alison

I feel like those things are externally focused. And that's where the disconnect happens.

There's a separation so that if I put all my attention in the external or outside world, I'm going to feel whole. I'm going to feel complete.

But it's not out there, it's actually within us. All of our perceptions are based on our beliefs and how we're looking [at it], what color glasses we're wearing.

Basically, what is the lens that we're looking through?

It wouldn't really matter what changed on the outside because the lens is the same. We have to look at the lens and tend to that.

So it's an introversion — an introverted experience. And within that, when we return to the scriptures, like when we read the Bible, we can see more clearly what it's actually pointing to. And again, it's pointing back to you the truth that you are divine, because you have been created in the image of God. You are God. God is all around us and within us.

Kelly
Therefore, you can affect your own universe. You have to stop feeling helpless and stop thinking you can't do anything about this. Exactly. You have all the power to do it — you have the power.

Alison
You <u>are</u> power. Yeah.

Kelly
I know we can't control if a car hits our car.

Alison
That happens....

Kelly
Right, but you can control everything that happens after that.

Alison
Exactly. You have how you feel about it, how you handle it, or if you're hurt and all of that. And so I don't believe I can make sure that a car never gets me.

Kelly
I think so many people just feel helpless. And that's my favorite

thing about my last year is learning that I'm not. And if I start feeling that way, you know, I can smack myself [figuratively].

Alison

Yeah, that victim consciousness. You're not a victim, that we're actually not victims. If we believe that we're a victim, then we are a victim.

We are empowered to not be that.

Sometimes when we have traumatic experiences, it's hard to shift from A to B. But that's why what you're doing here is really powerful, because it gives folks something to look out for and guide them.

Kelly

Well, you never know what one sentence literally changes somebody's life.

Speaking of that, let's talk about a lotus flower. Do you remember how you said it? Because I mean, I know I've messed it up, you're so much more eloquent.

The story behind it being, we're all together, we're all in a room [in Portugal on the Camino], a bunch of us are friends who kind of know each other. And then some are strangers, right? And we're all sharing why we were on the Camino…

Alison

That's right. You're very dynamic, you're very outgoing, you're very gregarious, you're very open. And, you are entertaining and laughing and just really bringing everyone in.

What I noticed was when a man was present, there was something that shifted in your body, in your way, and it felt a little more flirtatious. You're so open to meeting people, but with men specifically, you would always put yourself out there.

I was always impressed with that because I don't seem to have that ability. And I really admired that in you in that sense.

But what I noticed was more of an energetic shift in your body. And I thought that was so curious. And it was almost like you opened up in a different way. And there was just a different way in your body positioning and a different way in your energy. And it was like a flower opening up.

So whether it was a lotus or lily or a sunflower or whatever the visual was, I just had this feeling of this open flower and being receptive.

Kelly

I can remember how you said it to me — that it was a very kind and loving thing. It's almost like your motivation behind it, I don't know, but it felt like you wanted me to see that about myself.

Alison

Yeah. It was because it was so interesting that I felt like there was a seeking for something outside of yourself, to make you feel whole or to take away the pain that you're feeling.

Maybe you believed that if you could just find that right relationship, that right person, that other, that you wouldn't feel that sense of loss, betrayal, trauma, tragedy, devastation, heartbreak that you were wanting to let go of. But yet it was still very much in your experience of day to day life.

And the shift that would happen when men came into the realm that we were in, even just really casual, there was just a shift that happened. I felt like it was an unconscious shift.

And from that unconscious shift, it kind of tethered you to that belief that someone outside of you would help you feel whole and take away the pain that you were finding yourself still circulating in.

I know you weren't in there all the time, but I also know that you were mourning the loss of someone that you loved and so that just added to that whole piece.

But there was an intensity around what was coming as we were walking toward Santiago and the end of the Camino. There was an intensity of what was coming toward you in terms of calendar time and family engagement and what that was going to look like in terms of your friend Dan's funeral and your daughter's wedding. Knowing that you were going to have to face this thing.

And that was something I felt like you just didn't really want to face. You didn't want to go through that threshold.

I felt it was big and scary, like I would rather just not have to do that. If I could vote to not do that, I would not do it.

Kelly
I couldn't not go to [Dan's] funeral because of his girls.

Alison
Yeah, and it felt like a really important, courageous step you had to take. To step into and just to move in that direction — that it would actually free you if you could do it.

Kelly
Yeah, and it did, but it was just figuring out that I could.

I appreciate that you gave me that insight. My point of telling this story is you never know if you say something, if you see somebody struggling or even unconsciously doing something, you can give them that information — this is what I see.

Not accusatory. I think what stuck with me was how you did it and how lucky I was, how blessed I was that then I could see myself doing these things. And it helped me see my relationships differently with somebody that only responded to me if I was turning up the flirt.

I think now when I take it to the most basic level, I was giving my energy away because I was trying to attract energy unconsciously and subconsciously. I think the point is, from your side, you were able to lovingly give me that information without judging it. And from my side I received it without it hurting. Yes, well, it did a little.

Alison
Yeah. I know I can really have a strong effect on folks. I've learned to let it come out more softly, like more of a slow pour than a downpour.

I don't know if the words would have been any different. I think it's just the Shakti[5] that comes through. It's more like I'm observing my own expression.

---

[5] In Hinduism, especially Shaktism (a theological tradition of Hinduism), Shakti (Devanagari: शक्ति, IAST: Śakti; lit. "Energy, ability, strength, effort, power, capability"[1]) is the primordial cosmic energy, female in

Kelly

One of the first things I say in my book is, "I am no doctor, I'm no minister, I'm no therapist, I just want to share this with you."

When you hear something, when somebody shares something with you, honor that it was shared with you and hold it. Just hold it inside, maybe in a secret place, until you're ready to deal with it.

Or if somebody's noticing something about you then just accept it. It can be a year later, it can be five years later.

When somebody says something to you, don't dismiss it, because it might find a place in your healing going forward.

Alison

Beautiful.

Kelly

Thank God we're recording this. I'll never be able to say that again.

These couple of things were my big moments on the Camino. Did you have a big aha moment with the Camino?

Alison

For the Camino, initially, I was thinking, "I'm going to do this on my own, I don't want to be around people. This is going to be my retreat, my pilgrimage."

---

aspect, and represents the dynamic forces that are thought to move through the universe.[2] She is thought of as creative, sustaining, as well as destructive, and is sometimes referred to as auspicious source energy.

And what I realized is that I am not an island. And that actually, I rely on people all the time and I'm in community with people all the time. And there's this kind of attraction aversion thing that I do around that.

Actually, if I let go of the aversion part of it and acknowledge and engage with the relationship and being with others, it really feeds and supports the intention of moving forward.

So I really felt that the presence of the three of you, there with me together, was for my benefit in terms of even if nobody carried me, but we all carried each other. I really feel that we were there for one another, for whatever reason we came together.

I don't think I could have done the Camino on my own and maybe not have finished it. Maybe there would have been other people. Who knows? I just felt like that way of being with each other really helped me walk it.

Kelly
I really thought so too when I started out.

Last time I walked the Camino in Spain, in 2018, I found my Camino family really quickly and after a few days, I was with them all the time.

Yet, in Portugal with you all, I was mourning Dan.

I had found the new me and I really like her. I want to spend some time with her. I'm just going to do this by myself. This is going to be different.

I met Alice the first day and I also met you the first day. And Elsa the next day. And we met some other sweet, sweet people along the way as well. But yeah, I was gonna do it by myself.

Alison

I think that the interesting thing is that we were all going to do it on our own. And I never really felt like anyone was chomping at the bit to be on their own, that we were all in some way grateful to be together and also acknowledging that it was OK if we weren't in each other's pockets. There was this knowing and understanding that we're doing this on our own, in our own way, and we're all together in that experience.

Kelly

We're together even if we're not together.

I think that the first time around in 2018, I was just trying to absorb and learn from other people. And I was lucky I ended up with Bob who had hiked the Camino before.

Then this time around [2022], I felt like I WAS Bob. Right? So when you guys had questions, I knew the answers or knew how to find the answers. It felt good. It just felt good to know how to help you guys. And it was almost like a Camino give-back to me.

Alison

You were like our Camino mentor.

Kelly

Camino mom.

Alison

Yeah, it never felt like we were four individual people. It felt like we were a unit.

Kelly

OK, so down to the last four questions. What feeds your soul?

Alison

There are so many things that feed my soul.

The first thing that came to me was meditation. And the second thing that came to me was being in community, talking about yoga and being in yoga.

And then the next thing is nature.

There are so many things that feed my soul.

And I like the synopsis of that — it feels like everything can feed my soul. Even the most mundane things can feed my soul because it's how I show up for them.

It's not about whether they're good or bad, but how I am in response to what's being presented. So if I'm taking care of myself, nourishing that energy body that we're talking about, then everything is feeding me.

Kelly

Wow. I like that, teacher.

Next question: When you get sad, and most of us do get sad at some point, what do you do to self soothe?

Alison

Well, I actually just had a sadness. Where I grew up in South Florida, Fort Myers, was devastated by a hurricane. All the places that I love and hold close to my heart. Even though I haven't been there probably in close to 10 years, it is so viscerally immersed in my being that it is with me every day.

And the recognition now that those places, the actual structures that I have in my mind's eye, are no longer there, and they don't exist anymore. They've been destroyed.

So beaches and places — there's lots of memories around all of that and these places are gone. They're just completely wiped away.

And so the sadness with that is a mourning for sure.

I just do my best to acknowledge and give myself permission to feel it and try not to push it away or belittle it.

Acknowledge that I do my best to just really feel it, not even on an intellectual level, but on a visceral physical level.

I was in meditation with Gurudev, my guru, last Friday and I really felt the connection to these memories in relation to my mom.

I lived with my mother in Fort Myers and those memories have me holding on to that place. I was recognizing those places are now gone [because of the hurricane] except in my memory. I can't really hold on to them.

Does it make sense to hold on to the memories in the way that I have? I'm recognizing this is nature saying it's time to let go because the places don't exist anymore.

So you can have nice fond memories, but don't let that be what drives your decisions or guides you through your life. Because life is happening now. So I just felt these tears come and I just sat with that sadness. And I just let it be there like sitting in a pool of water. And it passed.

The sadness still comes back from time to time. Just sitting in it allowed me to let go of some of the energy around what I was feeling. Whereas if I hadn't sat with it, I feel like it just would continue to be kind of building there. And spinning on itself. I don't know if that makes sense.

Kelly
After you sat with it, are you able to take a deep breath and say I'm done? Or I'm moving on?

Is there anything specific that you do there? Or is there anything that you need to do after that?

Alison
Really, the pint of ice cream, sometimes it's ice cream.

Kelly
I'm not an ice cream person, but I'll eat a bag of chips!

Alison
Sometimes a hug feels appropriate. I feel like just really honoring when that time has come and it's time to move on. It's just really like an honoring; thank you for giving me the recognition to even just be with that and feel and for allowing that to move through. And for me, that's grace. That's the breath of God, the hand of God. There's just grace.

Kelly
OK, next question. What are you hopeful for?

Alison
I feel like my hopefulness is that I can continue to be healthy and vital.

And of course, I have prayers for humanity.

Seems like we're going through crazy times, I don't know, I think probably we have always gone through crazy times. But I pray for humanity that we can just love each other instead of being angry with each other. And that really starts with me.

So I pray that I can always remember to love when I'm in those hard moments, and just recognize that I want this to be different than it is.

And then sometimes the appropriate response is just relaxing and letting go. And then I feel, again, I just feel free, more free and more open and more vital.

Kelly
There's so much that letting go can fix. I'm totally simplifying. It's true.

The Dalai Lama would have a lot to say about that very complex tiny little sentence but there are so many things that literally are life changing by just letting them go.

Alison
The hard part in letting go is understanding the nature of mind. So when you understand why it's hard to let go, then it's like we've dissected the various aspects of how we hold on and why we hold on. But we don't actually have to understand in order to just let go.

I feel like it's easy and yet it's not. So understanding how to let go or where we get stuck is helpful. I just want it to be different than this and I recognize it's not.

Kelly
So simple and a way to just say OK, things in life are not how I want them to be and then just moving on.

If you're already in that practice before a trauma happens, it's probably very helpful.

When you get to the point where you have to let something go that's surrounded by trauma or caused by trauma, if you're not in that practice, it's hard.

I think I was like this, just holding on to my identity. I was caught up in being the wife, the mother, the daughter, that bible study student, track mom, soccer mom. That was my identity instead of my purpose.

Katherine Woodward Thomas says, in one of the lessons, your purpose is not what you do. Purpose is who you are.

And I was the opposite of that, because I thought everything I did was who I was. I think I would have loved myself a lot more if I could have stepped back like I do now.

Alison
We're always right where we're meant to be. I mean, all these lessons to get right here right now. Right?

Kelly
Yeah. And the last question is: Any last advice for people who are going through a big change?

Alison
Yeah, just be patient and gentle with yourself. And just love yourself. Nourish yourself. Be kind and loving to yourself.

What do we want from others?
We have to give it to ourselves first.

Yeah, the most important equation in the whole room.

Kelly

Yeah. How do you treat yourself?

Alison

That's the most important piece. Be kind and gentle.

Empowerment Practice 7: This Will Look Different Next Week

As we heard from Alison, her best friend gave her a piece of advice that continually helps her reframe a situation.

Her best friend said to her, "This is going to look different in a year."

Then she would even whittle it down to "This will look different next week."

It actually put things more in perspective for Alison and she was able to let go of the feeling that her pain, frustration or anger would be a permanent fixture in her life.

And then Alison asked me, "Have you considered the possibility that he went into a relationship with her because you needed to go out into your life and do something else?"

That absolutely reframed my pain as an opportunity. I was quite sure I would not have sold the company, would not hiked two caminos and I wouldn't be this strong woman I am now.

Your exercise for this chapter is to reframe a situation that has you stuck. What is going on in your life that is constantly on your mind?

Get out a pen and paper or open a blank document on your computer.

1. Write down the situation that has you stuck and the related emotion, whether that is pain, anger, humiliation, grief, abandonment or any other tough emotion.
2. Now, think to yourself, "This is going to look different next year." In fact, it is going to look different next week and maybe even today.
3. Let's pretend we are sitting together. How could I reframe your situation with a question? "Have you considered the possibility that....?"

   Write down your question. Really push yourself here. No one will know but you.

4. Now meditate on the question. Try to be still and repeat the question to yourself. Set a timer if you need to for five minutes or even more if you need that time.
5. Now attempt to answer the question. How can you reframe what this will look like next week and then next year?

This exercise is something I did many times. It took months for me to reframe my situation to my satisfaction but each time I did, it became easier and I felt more peace. I hope you will too.

"THERE IS A SEED PLANTED IN LOSS THAT CONTAINS THE HORIZON YOU ARE LONGING FOR." — TOKO-PA TURNER

CHAPTER 8:
GRIEF AND LOSS

Grief is defined in _On Grief and Grieving_ by two authors Elisabeth Kübler-Ross and David Kessler as having five stages: denial, anger, bargaining, depression and acceptance. They later added a sixth stage called finding meaning.

My personal experiences with grief are not identical to the stories you are about to hear. I am sure your personal experiences vary widely as well. I'd like to tell you a little bit about loss in my life. I lost all my grandparents at such a young age, I was too young to process it. It was in my thirties that I first faced death.

I lost a loved family member in 1998 to cancer. The family member fought bravely for five years and we were grateful for the time we had with her. It would never be enough but we were able to say our goodbyes. Having this opportunity lends itself to a different way of processing grief. Of course, this first major loss also taught me that time is not promised and about gratitude.

In 2008, another family member of mine experienced a traumatic accident that left them needing permanent care at the age of 50 and although they survived, it was an extremely difficult time for our family. We were so grateful he survived and our family pulled together to help him achieve his greatest possible independence, but it was also a time of deep grief and trauma in many lasting ways.

We all handle grief differently. I always thought I could handle crises well — make a plan and go forward. Taking action and rallying around people who need me has never been hard for me. My understanding of who I was in a crisis had always been the same, until I experienced the loss of my marriage. Then I froze. It was definitely the deepest grief I've ever felt up to that point. You have been reading about the processing of this grief throughout this book.

Then, in 2022, when I lost one of my lifelong friends, Dan, it was quite a shock. He was healthy and happy and living his dream of sailing Mexico in the winter. I joined his crew in November 2021 to compete in a sailing rally from San Diego to Mexico. As a first-time team, we came in second place in our division - I do have to brag for Dan.

During the 30-day sailing rally, we had a lot of time to reminisce but also to dream of the future. He encouraged me to write and tell the stories I had swimming around in my head and heart. I feel so blessed that I had that experience with him before he died.

His accident and death came right as I was embarking on my second Camino in Portugal. It was a tough way to grieve because I was alone and far away. But Dan was the one who encouraged me to walk my first Camino to heal from my divorce. Therefore, it was quite poignant that I was on the trail while grieving him. I felt him with me every day.

Coming home from that Camino, I felt a change in my grieving process. It wasn't about taking action anymore.

It was about letting the pain come to me on the trail, letting the tears wash away the sadness, and letting my laughter be the light and love I had for my friend.

I talked to him throughout and still talk to him almost every day. I can hear him answer, "You're doing great, Kel."

With this chapter, I want to acknowledge the important part that the grief process plays in our lives. There is no right or wrong way to do it. And there is relief and healing when we share the grief with others. *Grief is like water; the more you spread it around, the faster it evaporates.*

You just have to be IN IT.

You must walk THROUGH IT.

And then you must ACCEPT AND LET IT GO as best you can.

Timing is everything and grief is one of those challenges in life that has its own timeline. You move from one stage to another, but not in a straight line and you can go back and forth, forwards and backwards.

My friend Kaye shared with me, "Grief is like fingerprints — no two are alike, so trust where you are, claim it, and keep going."

I believe if you are reading this book, you are likely in one of the stages of grief, even if you don't necessarily have an obvious loss to point to. The loss that initiates grief is not always physical.

We can experience loss through death, but there is an infinite list of ways we can feel loss — loss of friendship, loss of physical capabilities, loss of a previous way of life or financial security, change in your health or a loved one's health, losing a job or opportunity.

I hope that you are at the acceptance stage or that you are working towards getting there. Maybe reading this chapter will help you in your grief journey if you are stuck.

I want you to hear from three women who have experienced and sought to overcome these stages of grief and I believe they have a lot to offer us, as spoken from their hearts and experiences.

Kayce's Story

My friend Kayce, who you hear from in other chapters, lost her son to suicide when he was at the tender age of 17. She was recently divorced and had one surviving child, a daughter.

Losing a child is every parent's fear and walking beside Kayce as she navigated her grief was an honor. She gracefully accepted help, she was honest when she needed alone time and she was ever-vigilant about putting her daughter's needs first.

I hope as you hear Kayce's story, you absorb how to accept help when you need it most.

Kayce
Before the loss, I had two beautiful kids, a boy and a girl. They were very close.

Sadly, my son suffered from major depression and suffered alone with that for several years. He finally told me about it at age 16, but by then the depression had really taken hold and it was tough to pull him out of it.

We started to get him treatment. It worked for a little while, but after just a year he took his own life. We knew our son was experiencing suicidal ideation, so we were watching him. But he was so high functioning, never missing a day of school, excelling in school and in his extracurricular activities and part of me thought he'd never actually go through with it.

Now I wonder if the divorce worked as a trigger.

I've learned that some people are wired for depression and then there's some kind of trauma that ignites the condition. It's both biological and biographical.

So if we hadn't split up, who knows what would have happened. But after my divorce, I came to find his father suffers from major depression. I never knew it. Never put words to it. I didn't know that's what it was at the time.

So it's especially difficult when you go through losing a child, and because of divorce, you're no longer with the other parent…the only other person who knows exactly how it feels.

So I was alone in that sense.

You don't lean on the surviving child because that's not their job. So, family and friends were crucial. I had been doing the dating thing on and off for a while, but wasn't seeing anyone seriously at the time.

After a few months, I needed the distraction and went back on the dating apps. I knew it was too soon, but I had no family where we were living and friends had their own lives…again, it was something to do to take my mind off my broken heart.

I remember my first date at that time, sitting at the bar in a restaurant with a very nice man.

I just kind of got it out early in the night that "this" happened to me recently. We're talking about kids and this and that and I remember I just started crying at the bar.

Right off the bat, he said, "It wasn't your fault. It wasn't your fault."

It was so comforting, this complete stranger, knowing me for 20 minutes, offering that response. And it being exactly what I needed to hear.

Kelly
He must have known. My guess is he was close with his mom.

Kayce
That made me cry even more because it was such a sweet thing to say. To his credit, he did ask me out again, even after that…something that would scare anyone away!

I have to say, all the gentlemen, it didn't scare anyone away, everyone was very sweet. I think there maybe were a couple of people I didn't share it with because I didn't sense it was going anywhere.

If you're really connecting with someone on a date, it almost feels dishonest to keep that in your pocket. Sometimes, it'd be the second or third date, but mostly I shared this early on just because it's such a profound, life-altering event. As I said, it almost felt dishonest to not share it pretty early on.

Kelly
Well, it's a life altering event. Like a divorce. Divorce is like a death, right? Yeah. I think that you were right and your instinct was very good there. How did it feel to say this? Was it a relief?

Kayce
Yeah, it was like, there's an opening in the conversation, this is a good time. "Something you should probably know about me, this happened…." I just never knew going in if I was going to mention it

or not, or when. But it was good to get it out if I could keep it together.

Kelly

Good. I mean, I think people would want to hear. Did you begin to share with your daughter about dating?

Kayce

When my son was alive, the first year I was dating, my children didn't want to hear a lot about it. I don't know that they were comfortable hearing about it much. I kind of sensed it and I took their cues.

I remember when I first told them I was going to start dating, they didn't like it from a safety standpoint. They didn't like the dating app concept…but this was 2015. A lot has changed since then! I remember my daughter saying, "But you don't know these people at all."

But then I think they started to see that I was happy and they were OK with it.

Kelly

I know it's hard to tell people. What were the varied reactions that were helpful or supportive to you after your son's death?

Kayce

I think it was those people who focused on helping me with blame. I remember I got two cards from people I didn't know. My son was in high school and it's a close-knit town. Everyone knew of his passing.

I received cards from two different moms from the high school, women I didn't know. They were complete strangers who shared so beautifully with me about the specter of depression in their own lives…either they had suffered from it, their child, their spouse, etc. They knew what it felt like to fight that beast. That was an enormous comfort to me…and the first time I experienced the vulnerability inherent in grief, that opens the door to forging closer relationships with people.

I remember one of the notes said something like, sometimes there is nothing else you can do to ameliorate their pain, when this happens, sometimes there's no explanation. You cannot blame yourself.

Both cards contained a similar message, I saved them. They comforted me quite a bit.

And other things that helped — just friends listening. Don't underestimate the power of chardonnay with one's girlfriends.

Good friends. Listening.

When somebody's going through something that big, you're better off just letting them process. That's what you guys did for me. So I had that support system. I don't know what would have happened. You guys saved me. You really did.

Kelly
I know the feeling. You guys totally saved me too.

June's Story

June, a beautiful soul and friend from a long-time series of bible studies in my church community, lost her husband Jason to cancer. He only lived three months from the time he was diagnosed. They had time to say goodbye, discuss financial matters, pray with friends and family and take time to be together as a family.

I hope as you hear from June, you learn how she reached out to her community. Before she ever had the diagnosis of her own husband, she was present for her friend whose husband had already been diagnosed. They had a mutually supportive friendship that deepened with the shared experience and means of seeking peace and comfort through cycling together.

June's story is terribly sad, but it is also so beautiful. I'll let her tell you.

Kelly
Tell me about your background and career.

June
I went to three colleges. The last one was for graduate school. I was a first-year physical therapy (PT) student and he [husband Jason] was a first-year med student. We lived in the same apartment complex and my PT class took Gross Anatomy and Neuroanatomy with the medical school.

Some friends of ours in his class, who were the social leaders, always invited the PT students to every social event to kind of balance out the gender because they had about 75 percent male out of 100 students, we had about 80 percent women out of 26 students.

So we met at [university] and that was in the fall of 1988. We started dating the next semester despite my very reluctant self. I was not planning to do that.

I was very career focused. I thought, 'I don't have time for this.' — least of all a med student who's going to have way more debt than me! I also thought that I wanted somebody who's not married to their job and there's so much of that in medicine.

We married in June of 1992 and then moved to Nashville for his internship in medicine. We were there for one year. I worked at a hospital and he was an intern.

I never saw him. He was on call every third or every other night. He was either post-call and just exhausted or could barely stay awake through dinner. One out of three nights would be sort of normal.

Thankfully, I had great work colleagues and found people to cycle with. I went to church. Jason was only able to go to church with me on maybe two Sundays that whole year. It was tough. When we went back to [university] for his residency for three years, we bought a house and had our first son. We moved back to Nashville in 1996.

We have four kids. Two are out of college and two younger ones are still in college.

Kelly
Tell me about Jason and when you heard the news.

June
I was working part time until Jason was diagnosed in October 2020. He was diagnosed with hepatic angiosarcoma. The first call we got after a CT scan was "It's not cancer, it's cirrhosis."

That was shocking and grievous, especially since Jason did not have the typical risk factors for cirrhosis.

But it wasn't that in the end. He had a biopsy that was sent to [renowned hospital] to get a clear answer because even the [original hospital] tumor board didn't agree that it was definitive. The [renowned hospital] pathologist diagnosed it and everybody at the [original hospital] agreed. When the word came back to us it was sometime in early October. It was a devastating diagnosis with an extremely poor prognosis.

Kelly
And it was cancer.

June
It was cancer, but not just cancer. It was a super-rare cancer of the blood vessels in the liver. So it wasn't liver cancer. It was a kind of sarcoma, which is also a weird kind of cancer.

His oncologist made a chemo treatment plan which was supposed to give him more time with us than he would have had without it, but that ended up not being the case. He was supposed to have six rounds of chemo, three weeks apart.

And after the third round, they did a CT which showed that there was improvement in the cancer, but his edema, symptoms and mobility were not improving. His liver function was not improving.

He passed away on Jan. 9 just three months after diagnosis.

Kelly
What were some of the things that people said or that people did which were helpful to you during this time?

June

One of the things that just saved my life was that my cycling friends, swim friends and church friends were all there for me to show up for and talk with. They all offered serious support and also held me accountable to show up for workouts or study, which was very important for me.

My good friend and training partner Sara, her husband had been diagnosed with a similar form of cancer in January 2020. We had been cycling together already. We'd been friends and training buddies for a while, but we were training together a lot already when he was diagnosed.

At that point I told her, "I'll be here for you whatever you need."

I scheduled my rides around her so she would have a riding partner for safety and a sounding board if she needed one.

When Jason got diagnosed, she poured all kinds of love on us and gave us all kinds of sweet gifts that were so beautifully thoughtful.

She invited our triathlon club or training friends to write us notes, she put them in a scroll and put them in a jar for us. When Jason first started chemo, we read a note per day. Some of them were from individuals and some were scriptures or helpful phrases. She gave me that in a blessing box that had other things too, like a book of imagery "escapes," a lavender candle, a note pad with inspirational quotes on each page. It was incredibly beautiful and generous.

My church small group of eight women were also a trusted and steadfast support system. One of them, named Sharon, hosted a beautiful prayer gathering in her backyard for many church friends and some of my family.

It was a free flowing of love, prayers, memories and encouragement from everyone. People spoke so much love into Jason and me and prayed out loud for him and us. Our friends who were church musicians also played inspirationally and led us in singing. It was all just so amazingly beautiful.

That was in the beginning, you know, and Jason got on his knees in front of everybody wearing a prayer shawl that was given to us that day. He shared about being so grateful for his life and his wife and just kept saying, "I've had such a good life. I've been so incredibly blessed. I'm here for a miracle and I'm here for healing. But if that's not what happens, I'm here for heaven."

He really meant it and it was amazing.

When Jason went in the hospital three days before he died, my friend Sharon had a prayer vigil in the front yard of our church. And there were probably 30 to 50 people.

Very dear church friends, Jason's colleagues came and some of my cycling friends were at the prayer vigil, despite it being planned and announced with very short notice. People showed up for him and it meant so much. She sent me pictures and a video, which I showed Jason and he appreciated, even in his somnolent state.

Kelly
How many people must have been so affected by Jason's words? That's like a gift from him to them, for them to be able to hold on to when something happens in their lives. It was a great example to be grateful even for the hard things.

I have a hard time with that and I've been working on it for several years. I mean, there's no why — there's just thank you for the things I'm learning right now. Don't ask why anymore.

June

Maybe at some point in my life I did, but it's been a long time since I believed that God ordains hardship. I definitely believe God can use it and that good can come from it. I definitely believe this. But I don't think that it was God's plan for Jason to suffer this way.

You've asked me what was helpful during that time. Every gesture of love and gifts and notes.
All of that is helpful and received as love.

Kelly

I know I fret about doing the right thing for my friends in these times.

June

I want to do the thing that they need the most or they want the most. Sometimes that's paralyzing and I end up not doing anything because I just don't know what is "best" to do.

People used so many different avenues to love on us. They gave us meal gift cards. There was a meal train where volunteers brought meals. We had gift cards galore to [meal delivery mobile apps] like GrubHub and UberEATS. And that was super helpful for us, you know? It just made it easy for us to not have to think about planning food.

Kelly

All the kids came home at some point right?

June

After Jason was diagnosed, they immediately came home for a long weekend. Alan had just been at college two months. He decided to move home because, with COVID, everything was online anyway.

And Drake moved home over Thanksgiving. So it was really Alan and Drake who lived at home with us.

They didn't all move home. Rick was in the area. Jillian went back to Boston because she had a job. They weren't really all here through all of it.

They were here for Christmas, though, and he was really sick through that December.

I told them all without scaring them that this is a time to lean in. If you're thinking about him, send him a text, send him a joke, something silly. But if you have time to lean in, this is the time to do that.

Kelly
The advice to lean in is great. Nobody has said those words yet. That's really helpful.

June
Cancer is so different from somebody being taken from you unexpectedly. I think it's a totally different experience. I started grieving in September with the erroneous cirrhosis diagnosis because that was pretty devastating. That would kill him.

So I really started grieving in September.

I would cry and just lay down in bed with him and put my hand on his back. I think a lot of my grieving happened before he died. I guess he did too, but he also just felt bad. Yet still he would say, "I feel great."

He would look terrible and he'd be really quiet when he was sick. We'd ask,"How are you? How are you feeling?"

He was an optimist. He often said, "I feel great. I feel better than I look."

Kelly
I like that.

June
I don't know if that was faking. He didn't fake anything, you know?

Kelly
Well, he's probably at that point when you're grateful for every day. You can will yourself to feel or not to feel a lot of things.

I think that's why grieving is important. And I think when you have time to say goodbye, even while they're sick, at least, you have time to say goodbye. It's a gift.

June
It is and that's one thing that my friend told me. She said, cancer is just like that – I wouldn't wish it on anyone but there is a blessing in it because it gives people time to show their love and time to say what they want to, and for the ill one to do the same.

Kelly
For those of us who were watching from far away, you could just see the love.

June
His [student] residents came and caroled to him one sunny day. He was known for leading the Christmas party at [hospital department] and so they arranged a surprise with me for them to come sing carols to him. That was one of the brightest lights for him.

One night later in December, the whole clinic staff and their families came and caroled to him in the backyard. He sat on the porch and they each came up, one at a time or a family at a time, to just say hello and get a picture with him. So that was amazing.

I could show you stacks of cards and notes. Even after he died, people that I didn't know wanted to tell me what he had meant to them, from patients of his to hospital administrators, they shared sweet stories and their gratitude for his life. Anyway, there's so much blessing in the love of people.

Now you're probably going to ask about dating or whatever.

Kelly
Where are you with the idea of dating? Just a wide open question.

June
In a nutshell. I am open to dating.

I had heard of the Hinge dating app and I have friends who met on it and I was curious so I listened to a podcast about it.

I'm content right now. Adding a dating lifestyle — I don't need that complexity added to my already-busy life.

I can see not wanting to grow old alone. But also I don't feel like I need that right now in my life. I don't need the complexity of emotional vulnerability. All the time, work, safety concerns and everything else that surrounds dating. That's how I feel at the moment.

Kelly
It does require a lot of time and attention and you have to be willing to be vulnerable, even when other people might not be being vulnerable. You have to be willing to do that.

You have to be brave, but I think time is the big thing. Time is a precious commodity. And that's what I would ask people — do you have the time and are you willing to give the time? If you're going to give your time, give it enough time to make it successful.

And are you ready to be vulnerable?

June
In the apps, you're setting yourself up for definite rejection — people are rejecting you as they accept somebody else all the time. You're being judged by very limited information about who you really are and you also are going on very little information in your judgment of someone else. I mean discernment more than I mean judge.

Kelly
I'm extremely discerning now — way more than I was [earlier on]. You can take it on a case-by-case basis. I have a friend who is hoping to find someone through all of her activities and not ever getting on an app.

June
Yes, I am open and hopeful for that, to meet someone naturally through the various activities and spaces I inhabit. It might be nice to be introduced to someone and just consider him as a friend. I don't need to immediately decide every time I meet someone if I could possibly land with this person long term or not.

I think eventually that will come up but I'm not going to enter every introduction that way. It's just different being introduced to somebody that you don't know already versus the whole app thing and texting/talking with multiple people.

Kelly

Everybody's different and it should be that way. Yeah, for sure. And then everybody hopefully gets accepted where they're at.

Sometimes you go into it thinking you're ready and then you think, "Oh, crap, I'm not" and you're right back out of that again. Or you'll date for a few weeks and then you're in need of a break. You can pause the dating app and take a minute.

Go have fun with your friends and then maybe three weeks later, you're ready to look at the app again. But I'm not afraid to turn it off or pause it or even sometimes just completely delete it. The problem with doing that is once you turn it back on, all those people you swiped left on the first pass, they come back around.

June

You have to do it again?

Kelly

And again. Yeah, they don't know you're doing it, but it takes time. So I learned to do the pause thing instead.

June

I was gonna add one more thing. Another part about my life that makes me feel content is my kids. We're very close and they're all still evolving as adults and I want to be available for them.

They've all had some crisis or another in their lives multiple times or whatever. And I just don't want to muddle that up right now.

I think if it is the right person, it wouldn't be a muddle and be just fine. But it's just another part of my life that adds to the complexity and also the priority. So I'm open, but I'm not longing.

Kelly

And you'll know when the time is right. I think that you're good at trusting your gut.

June

I feel so blessed to have had Jason. Jason was not perfect, and I'm definitely not perfect, and our marriage was not perfect. We had cyclical problems that came up and it just wasn't as perfect as you might think. I love him so much, but I also wasn't perfect.

I'm so thankful for our marriage and how it was in all its imperfection. And I'm so thankful for our kids and all of their imperfections. I don't feel like I missed out on anything. I think that's part of why I'm not longing.

I had a great marriage with an amazing partner and we have four beautiful, wonderful young adult children. It doesn't mean that I'm not lonely sometimes. I like the idea of having a partner in the future, but even if that never happens, I have already had an exceptionally loving, lively life in our family.

Kelly

I have to say there's no shame in being content. It's a beautiful, wonderful thing. Don't get shamed into dating either. That is your battle. It's hard. And if you're happy and stay happy, then maybe there's a day where you say, "Oh, I really would like to have someone — the kids are all good."

That's how I feel now. My kids are all so happy and so good right now. I mean, of course that isn't always the case, but right now they're good. And that's why I'm traveling and why I work so hard on myself. I've been doing all these workshops and meditations and praying like crazy and just feel free to do this right now.

I want somebody in my life and I'm willing to do the work to find that person. You have to have the time to invest in someone. It takes time to date. I'm busy with the book, but I'm flexible with the book.

OK. The first of the last four questions is what feeds your soul now?

June
The outdoors, nature. I am doing a course of study at [university] called the Tennessee Naturalist Program. I'm becoming a naturalist by learning, attending classes on different flora, fauna and other natural features in [Tennessee] State Park.

I love being in nature and I love learning about what I'm looking at. It's bringing all those things together. It requires 40 hours of classwork and 40 hours of volunteer work. I chose to get trained as a "trail friend" and that's what I'm choosing to do with my volunteer hours. I get to hang out at some of my favorite trails and answer questions about them.

Kelly
That's awesome.

June
I love my triathlon community. I'm in a part-time job with a race management company. My job is to help newcomers know what to do and know what to expect and prepare them for the race.

We have seven triathlons and they created a position for me called Race Concierge. I'm there for everyone who registers for our race but with the emphasis for first timers. I have prizes for them after they finish – it's so fun to see people achieve goals they set for themselves! That is just doing what I love, being outside, nature and triathlons.

Kelly

I love it. OK, when you get sad, and we all do, what do you do to self soothe?

June

I don't know if I do anything consciously to self soothe. I just kind of move through it. I let it happen.

It happened yesterday. I was drying my hair and I thought of something, which brought something very sweet and sad about Jason to my mind. I was drying my hair upside down and I just started crying. I just let it happen and then move on.

Kelly

I had another person say in an interview that the biggest gift I can give myself and

> the way to soothe myself was just to be with it,
> be in it for a moment and let myself feel it.

It's funny how some patterns are forming when I ask these questions.

What are you hopeful for?

June

I'm hopeful for? Oh, that's so loaded. For myself, a long healthy life.

Kelly

That's a good answer.

June

Because I know we're not guaranteed anything in the future. I'm also hopeful that my kids have healthy, happy lives. These are the struggle years, but I so hope and want that for them. I do think part of it is that if I'm around, that'll be better for them, especially since they've lost their dad.

Not because I'm so great! Just because I'm their mom and they need at least one parent to be around for those big milestone events.

Tanya's Story

Tanya is from South Africa and we met on the Camino de Santiago. She was young when her husband died suddenly in a motorcycle accident. She had young twins, a boy and a girl, and found herself alone.

Tanya thought she had an amazing life, happy marriage, cute kids and her husband's business was prosperous. She found out after his death that many lies were circulating around her, and her world quite literally came crashing down.

Tanya felt herself stuck in the anger stage of grief. She had an unconventional, wild ride of a recovery, literally. I hope her grit and determination inspire you to make hard choices and pull through your own tough moments.

I'll let her tell you this amazing story.

Kelly
Can you please share with us about your career highlights and especially how it relates to marriage?

Tanya
I've been a photographer since I was 18. I got married, had twins and put down my camera for two years. And when the twins were two, I picked up my camera. I set it up so my studio can go into a suitcase and could go anywhere. I started taking photographs again.

I was 34 and the twins were eight when Kenny died and it was nine days before my world came crashing down. I put down my camera again. I made the decision to take over his company, which was very foreign to me, being in the manufacturing industry, which I knew nothing about. All males and no females.

It took me a good two years to learn the industry and all the lingo that goes with it. Then I got a manager. I combined the photography studio and the company by buying a house and joining the two together.

So I did both simultaneously, left brain, right brain, left brain, right brain.

I held the company together until my son turned 18. So for 10 years, I was running both businesses simultaneously, changing the house into an office.

My son is now 34 and he's doing a brilliant job of running the company. Brilliant. He is growing and it's incredible.

I remarried when the twins were 10 to Toby and he was in corporate [work]. And 10 years ago, he left corporate, took a sabbatical and then joined me and my son at the company. So now the two of them are such a strong team. They really are brilliant together.

And then my daughter worked there for a while and then she got mixed up in the wrong crowds, got into drugs before she buggered off. I made her walk the Camino as rehab. She chose the Camino and the Camino started her healing process to love herself. That was one of her major problems.

She now loves herself, has become a vegan, teaches meditation and has finally found the love of her life at 34. And it is because of my daughter that I am changing now, getting into my spiritual quarter.

She came back to the business doing stock counts. She doesn't want to be in that space, but she's prepared to work and we'll pay her so she's getting an income. So that's all good.

Now I've got twins who are 34. And my son has given me a little grandson and he's six months old today. And, Toby has a grandson, my step-grandson in China. He's four. So two, one step grandchild and one grandchild of my own.

Kelly
OK, and Toby has a boy and a girl.

Tanya
Yes, and I have a boy and a girl. So we have four kids between us.

Kelly
OK. And how long have you been married now [to Toby]?

Tanya
It's soon to be 24 years.

Kelly
So, share with me about the experience of your husband's death. You know, you said the other day you felt like you were happily married and then there was a motorcycle accident, right?

Tanya
Yes. We had just come back from Greece where we celebrated our 10th wedding anniversary. Kenny took me back to where he proposed to me. We went up the hill to this little bench and the twins were saying, "So daddy, is this where you went on your knees? Show us how you did it."

And he even went on his knee and said this is where I proposed to your mother.

But afterwards I remember him running around like a chicken with his head cut off trying to get a phone connection with roaming. Think back 25 years ago when there was no roaming on your cell phone.

Once he got roaming, he was on the phone quite a lot. And when I asked who he was talking to, he said it was work for some clients.

And then I phoned my mother from the very same bench. And I said to her, "Mom, we're here at the bench where he proposed to me and it's lovely. We're having a wonderful time."

We walked hand in hand on the trip. We're having sex and everything was fine.

I was happy as ever, happy as a pig in shit. Anyway, it turned out I was a pig in shit literally. I was in such shit and I didn't even know it.

Later on I asked Kenny to sit with the kids while I went to buy earrings. He stayed there, but soon after I returned, Kenny unexpectedly said he had to go back home to run the factory because his father needed him. He left and I stayed in Greece.

Then my mother phoned to tell me that my dad is dying.

"Come home, come home," Mom said.

This was on Wednesday. And I said, "Mom, I'm on my way."

Hard to believe, but Kenny said to me don't come home. Your father's not dying.

But then why would my mother tell me that? My dad was in ICU with septicemia.

Later I found out why he didn't want me to come home — because he was taking the girlfriend away for the weekend and it would totally mess up his plan by me coming home.

I was on a remote island so it took me two days to get back to South Africa from Greece. I landed on Friday night. We went to the hospital on Saturday and I saw my father. And he was critical. He couldn't talk. He was really bad. And that's Saturday afternoon.

Kenny was a motorcycle-biker and he was cleaning his bike and he said, "Should I go on the breakfast run tomorrow?"

He always did that at 6 o'clock a.m. I said it was his decision.

I took him a cup of coffee while he was polishing the bike. And months later I saw the cup of coffee still in the garage sitting there from when he made the decision to go on the breakfast run.

The accident happened.

I don't know why I latched on to his briefcase and carried his briefcase wherever I went for about three days.

One night, nine days after he died, I opened the briefcase and there was this roll of paper. Back then 25 years ago, your itemized billing came in a roll. I opened this thing up and my eyes quickly picked up a pattern.

I got a highlighter and I started highlighting and there was my cell number, my house number, a different house number and a different cell number. And then I saw this pattern: No clients. There were no clients, nothing.

So I went to see who was the last person he called.

This is where it hurts — going back to that call. Now I see it on the cell phone bill. I see me calling my mother from Greece on the cell phone bill. Then I remember I said I'm going to get some earrings, please stay with the twins. We had just experienced the most romantic moment in 10 years.

And he phoned <u>her</u> [the other woman] while he was sitting in front of the twins. That one hurts.

Kelly
So it felt like your life was a lie?

Tanya
I would be swimming in the sea and I can recall that I looked at him and he's on his phone. And I'd come off the sea and he'd say he was talking to clients, but it was only her number. So he spoke to her the entire Greek holiday. And yeah, it really hurt.

Kelly
So you found out.

Tanya
So back then people put condolences in the newspaper.

I saw one condolence from Pam. I went to my best friend Pam and said, "Hey, why did you write that funny message in the newspaper." It said "Follow your brightest star. As always, Pam."

It's just so funny. I feel as if I am reading that message right now.

She said, "That's not me. Look below — there's one from me, my husband and my boys."

I even remember asking Kenny's brother, who's Pam?

Nobody could tell me who Pam was. And I was just so busy that I forgot about Pam.

So when I opened the cell phone bill and saw all these numbers, I was hopeless. So I phoned the house number.

A young girl answered. And I said hello and she asked, "Who do you want to speak to?"

To this day, I do not know how the name Pam came out of my mouth. Perhaps it was planted from the newspaper condolence.

And the young girl said, "She's not here, do you want her cell number?"

I wrote it down. And it was the same number as the one on the bill.

I called and an old woman answered, but in Afrikaans, not English. I thought, what do I say to that person?

I didn't know who this was and I didn't know what to say so I put the phone down.

I phoned his best friend. And I said, "Who the fuck is Pam?"

He said, "Oh shit. I'll be right there."

It was very, very weird because he was Kenny's best friend and he knew about all of this, I could tell.

He got on his motorbike and he drove over. He was with Kenny when he died. He held him when he bled out on the road. It was the most horrific accident. There was hardly a trace left of him.

Kelly
Just from the impact? Is that what you mean?

Tanya

Yeah, it was horrific.

So he told me she's the madame of the brothel house.

He told me he knew that Kenny had not used condoms at the brothel.

So he took me for an AIDS test on day 10 after my husband died. That freaked me out. I was called back by the doctor.

The doctor says Tanya, you have an STD called HPV and you need an operation. And I thought I was going to die. I didn't even know what he was talking about.

I had the operation and his family, the Greeks, just said he was crazy. Don't talk about it. My father-in-law said, "Just put it under the carpet. He's dead. Don't talk about it."

Kelly

HPV and you had to have surgery. I can't even imagine what that felt like.

Were you angry yet or were you just still in the denial phase?

Tanya

I felt dirty. I was shocked and in denial. I was robbed of the grief process and I carried this deep shame.

> How does this happen to me? I'm just a housewife.
> This doesn't happen to me.

It's like when you're 16 and you think you won't get pregnant. This is not going to happen to you.

I carried this shame alone, my horror story. We all kept it a secret.

I wore the required black mourning clothes for a year as the Greek traditions require. It was actually a relief to just rotate through the four black outfits and not have to think. But what they didn't know was that I was wearing every possible color of underwear that I could get my hands on.

Kelly
You were a good wife. You were a good mother.

Tanya
Yes. We went out. We cooked every night. We never fought. I mean I can remember ….

We were having sex one night and his erection just died. And he was holding his head and he's rocking on the bed. And I'm saying, "What's wrong, what's wrong?"

And he's saying, "It's not you. I love you."

He told me he loved me every day. Every day. His last words to me when he got on that bike that fateful morning. He tucked me in as I was sleeping and he said, "Goodbye I love you."

And he phoned me every day to see where I was. And then I discovered he had to find her and check where she was so that we didn't cross paths. And a year after he died, we had to go to the Greek cemetery and do the whole Greek one year ceremony — so many funerals.

One day, I just drove to the whore house. I had parked outside the house so many times, but I just didn't know what to say.

I knew she had been in my house while I was in Greece. He had played the domestic card, and he was cooking and she'd been in my bed. I just smashed all the plates and dishes and wondered if she drank out of them or did she eat off of them? I just smashed everything. It felt quite good to do that.

Kelly
That physical release. That's why a lot of people will ride a bike or go running or go hiking.

Tanya
Yeah, the release was actually lovely. The twins were small and they were sleeping. The house was a monster, a 1,000-square-meter house and I was alone in this place.

I'd lost nine kilos in two weeks. My throat just closed. I could not speak. I could not have this conversation with you for a good 10 years. I couldn't even talk about it. Nothing would come out of my mouth.

I went to a numerologist[6] who told me I had to write Kenny a letter and I wrote a 22-page letter and then burnt it. Later I planted the ashes of the letter in the plants and released it and then I moved on to the anger stages.

Kelly
At what point was this when you went to the numerologist?

---

[6] Numerologist: a person who conducts the study of numbers, as the figures designating the year of one's birth, to determine their supposed influence on one's life, future, etc

Tanya

It was 10 years after his death.

Kelly

OK, so the one year mark you drove to the whore house?

Tanya

When I drove down the driveway, she didn't recognize me, even though she had been in my house and seen my pictures. I said to her, "I'm Kenny's wife."

She was 15 years older than him. And she called me "my girly."

She said, "Oh my God. He loved you so much."

That it even came out of her mouth flabbergasted me.

So I said to her, "Well then why was he fucking you?"

And she says, "Baby, all men do."

And then I don't know what to even say back to that. The whole house had just been busted by the police and she was closing.

After that, I had to go back to the gynecologist and I had checkups for six months to get the disease clear. While I'm sitting in the waiting room, there was a quiz in a magazine that said "See if your husband is having an affair."

I realized I hadn't been able to see any of the signs. I had been so oblivious.

It said, he's lost weight. Yes. Tick that box. He has a change of clothes in his car. Yes, I ticked that box. He's got aftershave in his car. Yes, I tick that box. Yes. And I didn't see anything clearly. I was oblivious. I didn't see anything. So then after the anger…

Kelly

You found the grief stages: denial, anger, bargaining, depression. And finally acceptance.

Tanya

I eventually went into acceptance. It took so long for me to heal, not just 10 years. I wish I had gone to therapy and talked it out.

I took this course where the big question is "What do you want?" I really opened up and it was all about participation and, boy, did I participate on this course.

The first year, most people never came to actually visit me. They came to visit the poor widow. What you need is for people to lean in, but in my case people leaned out because of my anger.

Kelly, I swore so badly. Every second word was the F word. Neither of my twins use the F word. People would come visit me and I just swore and nobody ever came back.

People just disappeared and I was up there in the monster house.

The only people who leaned in were my mom, a new friend who stepped up and my husband's best friend. These three leaned in and got me through in three very different ways.

My parents had moved into the house with me because although my dad didn't die, he was critical. We nursed him for six months. That's how sick he was. It's a miracle he didn't die.

Kelly

You were talking about the course you took but you didn't say what was covered.

Tanya

It really did make me think.

You had to think about your sex life and when I said we had sex —
what I'm not saying is that it was not good sex.

I can remember lying there and thinking, "Oh, there's a plug on the
wall. I didn't know there was a plug on the wall."

We never watched porn. We never had any sex toys. We never did
anything adventurous. It was so boring.

This Israeli psychologist said to me, "Tanya, maybe you were a shit
fuck."

How's that, Kelly?

Kelly

I know. I had the same thoughts, but I did try to introduce fun
things into the sex life. We would do it and then he would never
initiate it again. So, yes, I think we were both boring.

Tanya

So maybe he went to [the other woman] for that. But then you
wonder why I got a disease. I want to vomit at the thought of all
this.

I remember being a shit fuck, actually remembering that one time
looking at the plugin. Yeah, I was really shocked looking back at
that night. You know, I was honest with myself, Kelly. And I
actually agreed with him on that.

But I didn't know any better.

I went to a sex toy party. All the girls ran in and bought up the
dildos and vibrators and I walked in and there wasn't much left

except this big dildo cock so I bought it because I thought I had to come out with a package. So I bought it and then I hid it in the garage.

When I walked in after the party, he said, "I hope you didn't buy anything."

And I just said, "No, I didn't buy anything." And then I took it back to the lady the next day.

So we had never done anything. He's screwing a whore, but I won't buy a vibrator?

Kelly
Well, I think that especially back then and it's maybe not that way now, but the wife was supposed to be pure and you weren't supposed to do those things. Some men wouldn't have a blow job or whatever because your wife is pure. This is the mother of my children and so they went elsewhere. It's OK to do "bad things" with the bad woman, but...

Tanya
But not with me. And I think he was like that. I do not deny he loved me. I absolutely know he loved me.

We never had fights. We never talked divorce. He was my best friend and we laughed. The sad thing is we laughed. I thought he was so funny. And we really, really were good friends and we laughed, but he had me on the pedestal.

Kelly
My takeaway from my marriage was that's not what I want when I experience this next love of my life.

Tanya

What I haven't told many people is that Kenny's friend, who was with him when he died, I had an affair with him for two years after Kenny passed.

He made me strong. He picked me up many times and made me strong. I rode that motorbike with him like a demon for two years. I rode with such strength and no fear. I would go 285 kilometers per hour on a motorbike with no fear.

Eventually, I had to come off. I thought, "I will be strawberry jam and my children will be orphans." But until then, I rode and rode and rode and rode.

But Kenny's friend was married and he said he was not getting divorced. He only let me just put a blanket over the pain.

Kelly

Both of you are having the affair.

Tanya

Yes. But I'm widowed and he's married. Right? Not that there's any excuse.

But I do not regret doing the affair. What I learned from him was that I didn't want to be a mistress, I wanted to be a wife.

Then I met Toby and I said to myself, "I'm going to go with Toby."

Kenny's friend and I were still friends and I spoke to him and he had many affairs after me. It carried on until I met Toby.

Kelly

Was it a good thing for you because it was the first time you really experienced not-shit sex? And he supported you and...

Tanya

It was. It was wild. You're rallying and partying and dancing and head banging to rock music and dressed in leathers. I wore this T-shirt that said 'Beware This Bitch Bites' and I was just fearless.

Kenny's friend was a naughty guy. And I was naughty with him. He brought out my naughty side. And my mojo was firing.

But one day I met Toby, this good guy.

Toby has accomplished a lot in his life even while carrying the burden of bipolar disorder. He was 14 when he first felt the changes. Winston Churchill referred to the symptoms as "the black dog appearing."

He has carried this black dog through his life and done the army, receiving the Sword of Honor from the president. He has accomplished so much.

He has carried this with him and sometimes feels shame as if it were a weakness. He didn't choose this. It runs in the family.

When I met him, he had been diagnosed with and treated for depression. He had been misdiagnosed. But kudos are really due for Toby.

He wasn't the man who planted the seeds of my kids, but he was the one who provided the water and the morals, values. And we have been through a lot with our four children, his and mine, and we have done it together.

I was actually warned by the doctor that this invisible disease can really pull a spouse down and I have had to fight some to keep my bubbly self going.

That's why I wanted to walk the Camino. I felt like I'd lost my mojo during my second marriage to Toby. Do you remember me telling you why I walked on the Camino? Two things that I wanted to find. One was my mojo. And the second one was I wanted to smoke a joint.

That's when Fifi, my fun personality, came out.

Kelly
That's when we met Fifi.

Tanya
She came out and you said, "Oh my god! All we needed to know was to give you a joint on day four."

I walked in pain with bad knees for the first 27 days of the Camino. When I smoked the joint, I was the dancing queen and I got the beers for everyone. It was so amazing. The pain just disappeared.

Kelly
Now it's such a great memory for all of us.

Tanya
Oh, that was so funny. Oh, man.

Kelly
You definitely connected with whatever that the marijuana did for you. It helped you let down and you were able to connect with the mojo part of yourself.

Tanya
Do you know when it was?

I remember walking one morning, the sun rose. I was alone. And I put my walking sticks down in the sun and I was standing there crying on my own. Just crying.

I had found my mojo. I started flirting. I haven't flirted in years. I didn't know how to flirt anymore.

Kelly
When do you feel like you were healed from what happened with Kenny?

Tanya
Only when I wrote the letter and something here in my throat released and then I could talk.

I can remember having a chest of drawers in my bedroom. I can remember putting in all this garbage. I opened the drawer and put it all in and set with my feet on it and pushed the bottom drawer.

And this is like the drawer opened, only 10 years later.

Kelly
It's interesting that you met and you married Toby and it was still four or five years later before we met.

Tanya
And how would I know if Toby was having an affair right now? I'm in the exact same position. I would not know. I never, ever thought Kenny would cheat on me.

And I never think Toby will cheat on me. But he did cheat on his first wife who he had the children with. But I just don't look at his phone like I never looked at Kenny's phone.

So I just trust the same way as I trusted so I feel like I haven't changed in that way. But I have changed in so many other important ways. I have loved each step of each individual change and I now find myself so very comfortable in my own body. I am comfortable with all the changes and I am more adventurous in the bedroom.

And let me tell you — you know I don't smoke. But I have marijuana toffees and they are a miracle. It's a tiny little toffee and if I have just a small piece Toby and I connect. I don't know why, but even he says we feel more in love when I'm stoned.

Isn't this the weirdest thing?

Kelly
Does he join you in taking the toffee?

Tanya
He doesn't because he takes his medications for his bipolar. He says no, they don't agree with him.

But he likes it when I have it. So if I have marijuana, that's the best time I connect with Toby.

Is that a harsh statement to say?

Kelly
You're just speaking your truth, Tanya.

Tanya
I'm speaking my truth. I love my husband. I find my husband very attractive — just more attractive when I'm stoned. I don't do it often. I might do it once a month and it only lasts for three hours and we have sex. I initiate sex now every time. He never initiates and it makes me cry.

Kelly

Have you talked to him about how you feel?

Tanya

Many, many, many times. He doesn't do anything. Nothing.

Kelly

I mean I'm glad that you can and that you're comfortable doing it and that you get pleasure out of it, I'm assuming.

Tanya

Yes and we have much more excitement when I'm stoned. We have a much more exciting sex life than Kenny and I ever had and I definitely am different. I can let my guard down in my head maybe.

I think sex comes from your brain. And I can release my brain when I've had marijuana. It just relaxes your brain.

Yeah, have you had marijuana and sex?

Kelly

No. I don't think so.

Tanya

You gotta try it maybe one time. And then phone me and tell me, "Tanya, you're not bullshitting. It sure is fun."

Kelly

Yeah, I've no doubt about that. I'm just busy trying to find somebody to actually have sex with!

But I get frisky when I'm drinking. It's the relaxing thing I believe. I don't really need the pot.

Tanya

I don't like drinking. So I mean, I've been on a wine tour hike. And the wine was the most disgusting part of the whole hike. I can't drink wine so I have one gin and tonic.

Kelly

What I like about your story is you had a non-traditional way of healing, or it seems that way to me. Do you feel like that? You said you definitely got to the acceptance, but it was the act of writing the letter. Because at the end of each chapter in my book, I have an exercise for the reader to do.

Tanya

You've got to write the letter. Find a photograph that you don't like of the person. Burn four candles, put a photograph in the middle then burn the letter, burn the photograph and use all the wax and then plant a plant.

And it felt like a white dove releasing. It was therapeutic.

Kelly

It's that writing letter thing. I've heard it over and over and over again. And it was a very healing practice, no matter which way you're doing it. There are a lot of different ways to do it. You need to do it for yourself and tailor it to the situation you're in.

Tanya

My brother said to me that I had to forgive him. He's very religious.

And he says, "You've got to get on your knees and forgive him."

It was about nine months after he died. I can remember kneeling down by my bed and saying, "OK, I forgive you."

But I know in my heart, I didn't mean it.

And I said, "OK, God, you can let him go up one rung on the ladder. He may not go to heaven yet, but I will give him a little bit."

Kelly
I forgive, but I'm not going to forget. And it was this year that I felt like I really did forgive. But I kept getting hung up on [the other woman] — I couldn't forgive her.

So the next question is: What feeds your soul?

Tanya
What feeds my soul is laughing with my daughter, laughing with my friends, going out, you know? After 25 years, I am not going to change Toby. We don't laugh.

Definitely laughter and I actually find joy at home. And I just like my own company. Yeah, I'm at peace at home. And that feeds my soul.

I love cooking. I cook every single night and it is with joy.

I water my garden with joy. And that feeds my soul to see my plants grow.

And it saddens me that the one thing my husband is lacking is laughter.

He's a very serious guy and he's not going to change. There's nothing I can do.

"You didn't marry a joker," he says to me. Yeah, yeah.

So I find my own happiness within myself. I don't look for it from somebody else.

Kelly
That's great advice.

OK, if you get sad, what do you do to self soothe?

Tanya
Well, maybe you'll find this surprising and unconventional but...I eat a toffee and masturbate.

I'm very, very, very good at self-pleasuring myself. I have mastered it because I watched a YouTube video of a 90-year-old woman named Betty Dodson. She is the most amazing woman. And you know, she says that before, it was like a dirty thing, taboo.

All women should go listen to her. I'm comfortable with myself because of her.

I watched her and I heard this woman talk openly about masturbation. She is 90. She has a good session with herself once a month now at 90.

I can love myself. I went on the Camino with myself. I can love myself and if he's not going to, I can initiate with myself.

Yeah. So that is very honest. And people don't talk about it.

Kelly
That's good. That's really good.

Tanya
And sometimes I can sort of just feel sometimes if I didn't initiate, he would go months without sex. Wouldn't even miss it. I don't even think he thinks about it. It's the weirdest thing. So I still think about it.

Kelly

Sorry, sometimes medications will do that to you.

Tanya

Yes. He's got no libido. But when I'm stoned, it makes him horny as well. So he taps in.

Do you know you get the munchies when you smoke a joint? He even gets the munchies.

You're really connected, man. You're connected even though I'm the one stoned.

I used to think I mustn't tell anybody. That's my secret.

Kelly

OK, what are you hopeful for?

Tanya

I'm an eternal romantic and I just keep thinking Toby will change. And I don't stop — 25 years and I haven't stopped hoping. I didn't divorce him, because I love him and he's a good guy. I just keep thinking he'll get romantic one day. And I'm bullshitting myself.

Kelly

What do you hope for outside of marriage?

Tanya

I'm just hopeful to have a wonderful relationship with my grandson. I am looking forward to doing things with him and hopefully we have a really good relationship.

I'm also hopeful for my country. I just hope my country can come right. I'm so scared for my country.

Kelly

Any advice for people going through a big change?

Tanya

You know, you got to be brutal with yourself.

Stop pussyfooting around thinking, "Oh poor me."

Don't do it.

> Challenge yourself. Be honest with yourself.
> You can't bullshit yourself.

Don't even try bullshitting yourself because your body knows when you are talking shit to yourself. Be honest with yourself and admit, maybe I did something wrong. Maybe I could have done this or maybe I could have done that. I don't know, maybe.

Kelly

Yeah. So first it is acceptance. And then challenge yourself.

Empowerment Practice 8: The Gift of Letter Writing

Many people use letter writing to express emotions. Sometimes that is a love letter, a Dear John letter and sometimes it is a way to relieve grief or pain.

I've been advised several times in my life to write a letter as a way of moving through a situation. I taught my children to use this powerful exercise and I believe it helped them at a young age learn to express emotions and find their words.

When I was grieving the loss of my marriage, I was advised by my life coach to write a letter to the woman my husband was involved with. Upon re-reading that letter, I saw a feeling of powerlessness in my words.

The perceived lack of control in the situation was haunting me and I had not seen that on my own until I wrote that letter. I was able to address that with the second letter of this exercise.

Remember, this is for you. No one needs to see this but you. Reading your own words is a powerful tool for recovery because you can identify the core of your needs.

Have pen and paper by your side or open a blank document on your computer.

1. Get to a safe and quiet place. Hopefully you have found your workshop in Chapter 4. Do what you need to do to feel safe. Is that a blanket wrapped around you? Is that making a

nest in your bed?

2. Write a letter to express your grief. Address your feelings of loss. That may be for a friend, a parent, a child, a spouse or a partner dear to you.

3. Once you have written the letter, create a phrase that makes sense for coping with/helping with this situation and use it as a mantra. For example,

    "All will be well"   "I take back my power"
    "I can move through this"   "I am beloved"
    "The best is yet to come"   "I release this pain"

    Now set a timer and meditate for 10 minutes. Be kind and loving to yourself in this space and allow the grief to rise up.

4. After your meditation, write a second letter. This letter is from the person you've lost and it's written to you. This person is sharing five things he/she loves about you.

    If it helps, think of the happiest moment with this person or a time before the loss. Write from this point of view about that moment. This person is writing to you about their love and gratitude for you.

5. If you choose, you can use Tanya's ritual and burn the letter as she suggested.

CHAPTER 9:
COMMUNITY: FIND YOUR PEOPLE

The older you become, the more aware you become that everyone is going through something. Everyone faces loneliness — especially when starting over and starting to date. Throw in an added layer of not having dated since you were in your twenties and the challenges seem more daunting.

Dating in its very base form is full of vulnerability. You are destined to receive rejection as well as having to reject a suitor.

This is why it is important to be in community with other like-minded individuals.

Being welcomed and being accepted by friends, new and old, is a vital part of recovering from big changes in life.

In the beginning, it can be important simply as a physical presence. Later, as friendships develop or deepen, the people around you can provide feedback, an honest assessment of the situation and a source of wisdom outside your own heart and mind.

"People need to feel loved and supported," says my friend Dolly, who we affectionately call our ring leader, our troop mom, our party planner.

Dolly has a knack for bringing people together, whether it be a watch party for a football game, a book club or a girls night out to see a local band. She has a talent for bringing different types of people together who are like-minded.

By now, you must realize I believe in the law of attraction. My friend Dolly is a master of putting out an air of generosity, inclusiveness and kindness. Those of us who love her also know we will always have honesty and straightforward advice from her and she knows we will reciprocate. We give to each other and we receive the like.

Seeking Joy

I recently read *The Book of Joy: Lasting Happiness in a Changing World* by the Dalai Lama, Desmond Tutu and narrated by Douglas Abrams. The book is a conversation where two world leaders come together to discuss the most important topic of joy.

This is where I first learned of the concept of Ubuntu, an African way of life, which means to have interdependence on each other.

"A person is a person through another person," said Tutu in *The Book of Joy.*

Tutu shares that we don't exist without two people coming together as parents. We don't learn to talk or walk without other humans.

"We belong in a delicate network. It is actually quite profound," said Tutu.

He goes on to explain that the village residents believe this so deeply that their greeting is "How are we?" instead of the Western greeting of "How are you?"

Also in this book, the Dalai Lama shared the lesson of Mudita, the concept of sympathetic joy. It is one of the Four Immeasurables of Buddhism which also include loving-kindness, compassion and equanimity.

Jinpa, the translator in the book, explains that

> "Mudita recognizes that life is not a zero-sum game, that there is not just one slice of cake in which someone else's taking more means we get less. Mudita sees joy as limitless."

For me these two concepts tie together the community that supports and uplifts a person in need.

Can we feel so connected that we understand that how you feel affects me?

Can we connect on a level where I am always happy for you and your success, your love and your wealth as if it were my own?

If we feel this connection and this lack of envy, there is a natural outgrowth of compassion.

I have known my friend Dolly since middle school as we grew up in the same hometown. We reconnected after we both were divorced and had moved to the same apartment complex.

From across the pool, I heard, "Kelly, is that you?"

We realized we had been through the same downsizing process over the last year. We have spent a lot of time together since then, even traveling to Italy together this year.

Dolly Interview

Dolly has a true gift for connection and so I asked her to be part of this chapter and share her experience. I hope you will be inspired to build and grow your own community of like-minded souls.

Kelly

What would you like to share about your background?

Dolly

I have a degree in Hotel and Restaurant Management. I spent about 10 years in the hospitality industry and I was able to meet a lot of different people.

One client of mine recruited me to [global corporation]. I accepted that position. And I spent over 25 years working for them. I was in a lot of different leadership positions both from the sales and operational side of it.

I was general manager responsible for very large geography, keeping people motivated and focused on client services and account management. I spent a lot of time on the operational side working with managers and employees that were critical in serving clients at their locations.

I had to find a lot of ways for them to stay connected and motivated because often they felt like they were part of our client's community and not our company's community. That job required a lot of travel.

During this time, I was married and in the [global corporation] years, I went through divorce. I did not have children. My choice not to have children was really specific to being a career person and trying to find a way to balance it all with my demands, my family situation or marital situation, the roles and responsibilities that I had to our family unit.

I knew that if I had children, it would be that much more on me. I was able to enjoy my dear lifetime friends' children and play critical roles in their lives and get that fulfillment. I offered to help my friends because it does take a lot to raise children in today's environment and the support that's required and the balance that families need within all of this.

Kelly
OK, so your first marriage was when you were in the hotel business and your second one was while you were with [global corporation]?

Dolly
I was working for [global corporation] both times. I was single up until my early 30s. I probably started seeing him (first husband) in that transition from the hotel to [global corporation].

Kelly
OK. And you grew up in Tennessee?

Dolly
Born and raised in Tennessee. I was able to stay in Tennessee and stay in Nashville. It's sort of like I grew up with Nashville as it grew up and the career opportunities progressed. I've lived across all of Tennessee, East, Middle and West Tennessee and I think it's a great state.

Kelly

You shared with me that when you were 41, you decided that you would not have children? Right? What was that decision like for you emotionally?

Dolly

I spent a lot of time with children as I was growing up. I was the community neighborhood babysitter. I helped with babies from the time they were born. I helped bring up several children in one family, twin boys at 11 and an 18 month old. I would be able to play basketball with them while I had the 18 month old on my hip and the others were around playing. I could juggle children very, very easily.

I guess I'd say I was in high demand as a good babysitter and offered a lot of support to those families, but I had always thought I would have children — always longed for children. That was just sort of my destiny.

I went through my different relationships. I had a college boyfriend that I was engaged to, but that marriage didn't occur. I had turned down a job two weeks before the engagement was called off. I went back begging for that job. That sort of pushed me more into a career person. I didn't expect it but that career continued to progress.

When I realized things in my first marriage weren't right, I knew I didn't need to bring children in the mix of this when it's probably not going to work out. I discovered some things [and moved on].

From there, I met a wonderful man. And I thought, 'Wow, this will be it.' This is my guy and we thought we were going to walk in that path with children.

When reality hit and I knew it just wasn't going to work out, I realized that I didn't need to bring children into this if there wasn't going to be a partnership and sharing roles and responsibilities. It was very difficult.

Kelly
You had a moment where you made that decision?

Dolly
Yes. I had friends ask me after the divorce. I can remember the day and the moment and where we were, some five or six women, and they asked, "Now, Dolly, did you ever want children?"

I actually became very emotional at that question because it was so hard for me. But they were so supportive and could understand where I was coming from.

And so it was a reality that I faced — it was not going to be in my cards and that was OK. During that conversation, I shared my true feelings about really wanting children and that being something very hard to talk about.

But I realized how many wonderful young people that I was involved with through my dear friends and their children, and the support that they needed and the things that I needed to do for my own family. I was able to reap the rewards of having children in my life and also give back to people that have been so wonderful in my world. So I moved forward.

Kelly
How about your family, your mom, your dad and your siblings?

Did they support you in that decision? Or did you really talk to them about it?

Dolly

I never had pressure from my family about having children. They left that decision up to me. They did know I really wanted them. And with the second husband, I think they really thought that was going to be a viable scenario. And of course, we all thought we'd have children, but it just didn't make sense.

And so from that aspect, I just moved forward and found my way to share my gifts. I love God and God has been good to me. He's guided me and he knew that my gifts could be served in sharing my love with young people in different ways and in different aspects.

Kelly

One reason your friends all love you is because you're such a good connector.

Dolly

Yeah. "Julie the cruise director" and they also call me "Scout Master."

Kelly

So tell me about how you create community, how you build community.

Dolly

I naturally enjoy meeting new people, getting involved in community.

My family has always been involved in their communities wherever we lived, supporting different school system initiatives. Education was very, very important in my family. And so they always encouraged us to be engaged and involved in community activities.

Being in team sports, being in dance activities, being involved in church community activities, being involved in school activities, serving on university alumni boards — just to be involved in the community. It does give back and a lot of it's centered around education.

So for me, I had great role models. My parents were phenomenal role models for me and what they engaged in from the community aspect.

I'm also a person that adores people. Because I had the time and I needed activities outside of my work, and I didn't have children. So I looked for things that I could get involved in and volunteer.

One thing I've always been passionate about is supporting young womens' careers. Because I'm so blessed to have some phenomenally talented women as bosses and leaders for me and they were always willing to help me and guide me. I had that both in the hospitality industry and in Fortune 500 corporations.

I was looking for a way to give back and so I engaged in some initiatives years ago at [a local] university, and then I re-engaged in that more recently. So I'm engaged with supporting 100-plus young women in their education and their careers and different activities that they're involved in.

> But when I meet people, I think about what's going on and how can I be a good friend?
> How can I cultivate that friendship?

As I get to know them and I learn about individuals, there are different things that I think would be supportive or beneficial.

Sometimes it's just an introduction and then I'll let them kind of go from there. I've run across a lot of women who have gone through divorces, who've been single moms taking on responsibilities. And I've found where there's a lot in common.

Everybody has something that they're dealing with and so how do we create a sense of belonging? I see that a lot of people are lonely at this stage. They've become empty nesters. The children are going on without them. And everybody's longing to be with someone and most would like a relationship, one-on-one with someone. But it's a little bit more challenging, a little bit more difficult.

And so creating that sense of belonging, creating those friendships, connecting those people and finding ways to it. It feeds individual souls and they aren't as lonely.

They identify. They start to understand it's not just them. They start to find joy and happiness and laughter and they start to realize that they can also help. They think, "How can I help?"

I'm going to use an example. There's a lady that I've known for over 20 years and she has been very specific about wanting to be married again. She wants that married life because she so enjoyed it. But recently she said, "I still want, that but I'm really really enjoying who I am, what I'm getting involved in and what I'm doing."

She thought, "I don't necessarily want to give up my friend group because I'm having such a good time."

We find laughter and laughter is good for the soul.

When I'm the connector, I have one rule. I will say you must be positive in the group.

Kelly
My next question — what are the qualities you seek out in your community of friends?

Dolly
I'm pretty adamant about positivity. For example, I was doing half marathon training. I needed a personal goal and somebody got me into doing half marathons.

I said, "Why don't we create a community where on Saturday mornings we gather to train for the marathon in the freezing cold, sometimes there'll be snow on the ground. Let's create our long walks and support each other."

And then we could have coffee and water afterwards and visit. And so people wanted to join that group and I told them I'm absolutely happy for you to be a part of that group. I said I just have one rule.

I said, if you go on the walk, you have to be positive. That said, you can go as long as you want. If you need to leave for an appointment or if you need to get somebody somewhere, you can peel off and come back. You just have to be positive on the trail.

It created so much joy and happiness for people that it continued to grow. People wanted to continue to be a part of that.

Everybody has challenges and everybody has negative things they're dealing with. Creating a positive environment, bringing a smile and being accepting of others — and their different things they have going on — it's just a powerful healing. It becomes a great support system that creates that community which generates love and kindness. I'm a big believer in 'Love Thy Neighbor' to bring the positive spirit.

Kelly

What are some activities that you enjoy when you and friends are staying in?

Dolly

I like having people over and I'll cook. We have appetizers or we'll have dinner. We have a book club I'm involved in. The book club is a quite interesting group of women.

We have game nights. We work puzzles. We do things like that especially in the winter months when it's harder to get outside. We'll watch football games — create a watch party for the NFL on Sundays.

I have a group of individuals that we've been getting together for at least the last three or four years. Everybody has a natural role. Somebody will come in and say, "Can I start the fire pit for you Dolly, please? Can I grill the steaks for you or cook the fish?"

Yes, please!

We have a friend that loves to host trivia nights and we have an app called Kahoot! that will create trivia questions and he will lead it. Same friend also has a game he made up that we love to play.

Kelly

Do you find when you do things like that the laughter makes you bond?

Dolly

Oh yes, laughter and music are so good for the soul. And you know, the Halloween party this year, we had about 30 to 40 people. And then we had a Titans watch party on Sunday [the next day]. And we had about 20 of those 40 people who wanted to be back together.

And someone says, "I feel like we haven't left the party since last night!"

We were still together and everybody was enjoying it.

It's amazing to bring people together. And then bringing in new people is pretty incredible.

There were some individuals that were new to this group that have different life challenges. Because they felt welcome, they felt comfortable enough in a very short period of time to express their need for ongoing support.

There are already connections occurring to support that person. This one friend is going to take the new friend out to play golf and get them going in different directions. They have a real need and it's pretty dynamic. And that's what comes out of a Halloween party — such a connection.

Kelly
What are some of the 'going out' things that you do?

Dolly
We go to football games (college and pro). Some of our group continue to go hiking in the parks. In the spring, they'll do these hikes for the wildflowers and a guide will show you the different wildflowers.

We will do community service. Some of us have helped a nonprofit called Rise Up for Hunger. We've done 5K races over the years. Of course, book club. One time we did a wine tasting based around the book that we read.

Kelly

We, of course, must say live music because you're in Nashville.

Dolly

Yes! Don't forget my live music. Yeah, definitely live music — watching concerts. We'll go to concerts. We went to Sting this year. About eight of us went.

We'll go to the lake and go out on the boats, maybe rent a houseboat and spend the night out.

But it's amazing — the community!

Kelly

Talk to me about how laughter plays a part in your life and your friendships.

Dolly

Look, laughter is good for the soul. It's healing and it brings joy, brings smiles and makes it easy for people to want to be a part of your group.

Kelly

Talk about how you and your friends formed the text group and how that has evolved.

Dolly

It's a <u>WhatsApp</u> text group. It started because someone took a trip and we created a little WhatsApp so we can stay apprised of the trip.

When you and I were in Italy, people wanted to know how things were going and to keep apprised. There were funny things that we would find along the trip and so I'd share. People want to be a part of something and they want to feel connected.

We go to work and it can be a grind. When we share within the group, we can create a little humor for people — something to laugh at or something that's out of the ordinary or just a surprise.

Someone says, "Look what I've seen" or "I saw this," and it just keeps the connection going for people during their days.

Kelly
And you create a good moment.

Dolly
Yes! You try to find two or three things in your day when you can compliment someone because giving a compliment warms not only the person you're sharing it with but there is warmth that comes into your heart. To do something positive. To help someone.

> That giving spirit just multiplies.
> It multiplies and it's captivating.

I have a couple of group texts. I have a book club group text and we wish people happy birthday. We remember their anniversary. Happy Friday, Happy Wednesday. I mean, people find a way to spread that joy just with those different little simple things.

Kelly
What brings you joy?

Dolly
Hmm. So, it's interesting as we get older, nests get smaller. The joy I get is having my friends together and then finding joy with one another.

The example that comes to my mind is, we have a Saturday Halloween party, I had company from out of town on Friday, and I was helping a friend create their Halloween costume on Thursday and had book club on Tuesday. And then we had the Halloween party and I played a big role in that.

So basically, the whole week was really busy. And I could have stayed in bed on Sunday and just rested and relaxed and all that kind of good stuff. But I knew in my heart of hearts I could not let my community down because they wanted to all be together for the Titans.

So my joy is when the group gets together and everybody finds happiness and support and then I hear about it through others about what it meant to them. I had one friend come to me and say that she didn't want to mess things up in this group. It was a very positive group. It was very drama free. And it meant a whole lot to her. And she shared that with someone else who was new in the group.

She said, "This is a pretty dynamic group that I want to be a part of."

So that, in and of itself, was joy.

And then another friend has been going through struggles around her marital life and she has felt comfortable confiding in me about the progress that they're making and they're staying together. But this community group has been there as she's gone through the thought process and supporting her and giving her the pros and the cons of ending or not.

To me, that speaks loudly of how the group supports one another. But to see the positive outcomes and the new friendships formed...that's joy.

Kelly

It sounds like trust, joy, laughter, loyalty. This sounds like all good things that are coming out of community.

It is interesting how all your different friend groups come together in different ways. And it's not all of them at the same time. It's beautiful.

So when you're having a bad day, what do you do to self soothe?

Dolly

So my first thing is to accept, recognize and identify that it's OK to have a bad day. And I do have my bad days.

I've put myself out there willing to be vulnerable and open about it and just say I'm not having too good of a day. And I then recognize it and accept it. Then I'll move through it because I know the sun comes up the next day and it will be OK.

To soothe my soul, I might just need to rest. I might be tired and I might need to rest. I might need to just get into a movie on TV, Netflix binge watching scenario. Find a happy movie that warms my heart. Sometimes it might just be to read my book or sometimes I might eat.

But I grant myself grace to have a bad day and know it's gonna get better and people will call and check in on you.

Sometimes I want to take the call. Sometimes I don't. I just need that quiet time. And sometimes I will talk to God and just say, I'm having a rough day.

That quiet time is phenomenal reflection time. It's hard. It's difficult. But some of the best stuff comes from those quiet days. And you grow as a person, you become stronger and you actually have some of the best ideas that move you forward in a good place.

Kelly
What are you hopeful for?

Dolly
I'm so hopeful that I can keep the community going forward. Hopeful for a relationship.

I'm hopeful for great things for my friends. For my family.

I'm a person who gets tremendous joy when phenomenal things happen for my friends. So when I start to connect people, part of that connection is I can see something that would be helpful or hopeful that would be an outcome for them.

You know, the easiest example is I have a new realtor friend. Well, I was hopeful to introduce her to someone that might help her prosper in her career.

I introduced another set of lady friends and both of them had been friends of mine for 20 plus years. And I knew them both so well. And they were within a year or two of age and for two years. I tried to get them connected. I kept saying y'all have to meet. Y'all are so similar. And the outcome of that was they became really dear friends.

So I was hopeful for that two year period to get these two individuals connected and that there will be a positive joy and outcome to those friends — creating a new friendship and a support system.

They support one another and it's pretty incredible how they have helped each other.

Kelly

What advice do you have for people going through a big life change?

Dolly

Grant yourself grace for what you're going through. Accept and know that you're normal.

> Know that you're not alone. Know that there is support and help for you and that it's OK to ask for help.

That's a big one. Sometimes it's hard to admit needing help but people will surround you with love and joy and support in so many dynamic ways when you let them in. So let people in.

Find things that bring you joy and treat yourself. For myself, the mani pedi makes me feel great. Getting up and getting dressed makes me feel great.

Time has a way of healing. Every circumstance is different. The timeline is different for everyone. So grant yourself grace to have good days and bad days. There's so much support and love out there and let it in.

Find your people. Find your community.

Kelly

I love that. There's so much love and grace out there.

Shania Interview Part 2

Trust and Open Up

From our conversation in Chapter 3, Shania and I talk about fighting for what you want. In that conversation, she also spoke of trusting and opening up. Here's a short excerpt that I think will be helpful.

Kelly
Well, let's just go back and talk about the path.

Shania
We were talking about the reason you're able to write this book, the reason you're able to have these interviews or even have all these strong women in your life is because you were willing to share yourself with them.

You said you had already formed these trusting relationships so when you went into this rough time, you felt comfortable. And that's true for sure, I mean how many times a week did we see each other? You also made some new relationships with people.

Some of the people that you are interviewing are not long-term people. With these people, you went into those relationships willing to share — share the ugly sides of your life.

I think so many times we aren't offering the truth.

Sometimes it's just about social norms. You just don't go out saying, "Hi, how's your day? I've had a really sucky day."

You just don't start conversations with the bad stuff. Right?

And so I personally have had struggles in my life and I have no problem sharing them, but I look for opportunities when they're going to be received. I am not going to a dinner party to share.

Well, you know what though, I've been at a dinner party and I shared my ugly parts if that's what that person needs. But I don't know you need it until you tell me. I think that's common in society.

When Brené Brown says "daring greatly" she's saying, "You need to be vulnerable."

And when you're vulnerable people respond to that. I think this is what you've done in this whole experience is you show people your vulnerability. Another way she says it is, "You allow yourself to be seen."

Kelly
I just looked up this passage from a book called *Pilgrim Strong: Rewriting My Story on the Way of St. James* by Steve Watkins, a man who walked the Camino de Santiago. I read this book before I left for the Camino in 2018.

We were talking about one of the reasons I was able to share with you and my other friends was because we were already friends. Right.

But going on the Camino, I was planning on being alone.

But then it's like everybody is there for a reason and has a problem. John Brierley, who writes a lot of the Camino books says, "You come with a question."

Even if you don't know you have a question, you have a question. There's a reason that you're there.

I didn't even know how to answer when people would say, "Why are you here?"

It would take me half an hour to say it and it eventually got down to an elevator speech of, "My husband cheated on me for six years and I'm here to start over."

Yeah, that was my elevator speech. That was my Camino line. But it took me a few weeks walking the Camino and talking to people to drill it down to that as to why I'm here.

I'm here to start over.

But Steve Watkins, who wrote this book, said,

"When you're alongside someone who's freely decided to walk 500 miles, respect is often the first feeling you have toward them. That's a good beginning. There were countless occasions on Camino when I'd easily spend more time in a day talking with a fellow pilgrim than with a friend back home during an entire year. Few topics were off limits."
<u>Pilgrim Strong: Rewriting My Story on the Way of St. James</u> -- **Steve Watkins**

That's what you reminded me of when you said this. The line from that book — I keep it bookmarked. When somebody asks me about the Camino, I read that to them because even if you're the type of person who's not super open, it's easy to be open there.

Here's the spoiler alert. "The Camino" means "the way."

The way is the path and what you learn is you've always been on this path, you'll always be on this path. This is your path.

The thing to learn before it's too late and there are regrets, because I don't want anybody to have regrets, is these resources of friendship and kindness and love and vulnerability and acceptance are available to you.

You have to look for them and accept them.

Empowerment Practice 9: Connection is Key

Dolly is the queen of connection and provided some great examples. This exercise is about stepping out of your box and stretching your wings.

When I separated from my husband, I needed to move. I had decided to hike the Camino at that point so I joined some hiking groups on <u>Meetup</u>. This is a local app where interest groups can connect. Even still, hiking and running were great, but they weren't enough.

The lonely quiet evenings were killer for me. So I started exploring Meetups for things other than hiking. I saw dancing. OH. MY. GOSH. I love dancing and the thought of getting lost on the dance floor sounded perfect.

I put on my dancing shoes and went to free salsa dance lessons I found online. I figured, hey, I'm going to Spain. Why not learn to salsa?

So I encourage you to lean on your existing community but also lean in to a new challenge to meet new people and try new things. Stepping out of your comfort zone, your neighborhood, your gym, whatever…it will help you in a unique way. You will be proud of yourself — even if you can't salsa (because that was me).

The challenge is to browse, peruse and explore the thought of doing new things. And I challenge you to take one step more. Sign up for something new.

1. Meetup is a connection website service that you can access online or in the app.
   o Outdoor activity groups are easy to find.
   o Foodie groups are fun!
   o There are specific groups for men, women or co-ed.
   o Just search for what you are interested in and you will find a group!

2. Local libraries have amazing classes and some are free!
   o Want to try new computer skills?
   o Sometimes they will host speakers about traveling.
   o You can volunteer to help with the book returns or shelving books.

3. Volunteer in the community. Do something that makes you feel like you are giving back. Giving to others is one of the healthiest ways to heal yourself.
   o Homeless shelters always need help or supplies.
   o Local churches usually have outreach programs to serve under-served populations.
   o Tutor underprivileged children.
   o Volunteer at a Boys and Girls Club or a local YMCA after school program.

4. Volunteer at a local animal shelter. They need help with dog walking and supplies.

5. Join a church or cultural club such as a book club or a wine tasting club.

6. Take a clue from Dolly and just start inviting people to do things together. Game nights, sporting events, trivia nights — anything works! Just do it.

The new you is out there and you are fabulous. Go get 'em!

DON'T TRY TO CHANGE PEOPLE. MAKE A REALISTIC DECISION
ABOUT WHERE THEY FIT IN YOUR LIFE BASED ON WHO THEY ARE,
NOT WHO YOU WANT THEM TO BE. — TINYBUDDHA.COM

CHAPTER 10:
BELIEVE THEM THE FIRST TIME

In a world where texting is the norm (over speaking) and sarcasm runs rampant, how are we supposed to decipher what is happening in a relationship? We read other meanings into words in a text or we miss completely what someone is trying to say.

Kayce gave me some great advice one night.

I'd gone on a first date and the guy, Sam, told me he was an asshole, he was broke and he was also a chauvinist. Well, I'd never had anyone say these words to me — most men deny it — so I thought he was joking. Go ahead — laugh. I DO!

The next day, I'm having a glass of wine with Kayce and she shares a quote from Maya Angelou that says

> *"When people show you who they are,*
> *believe them the first time."*

I guess in all my naivete and just being used to family sarcasm, I chose to believe he was just being self-deprecating. He wasn't. He was all those things. I won't say I wasted my time because I learned valuable lessons, but...

Listen to Maya!

Another example. I met Blake on Bumble. He was in town for a wedding and we decided to meet. We clicked on a fun level, an emotional level and a chemistry level, but we also had some similar tough experiences in our life that brought us close quickly.

We ended up having four dates in one weekend. This was so good for me in many ways because I was able to be completely open with him and he helped me feel like a desirable woman. But he did not want a long-distance relationship.

I have seen how long-distance relationships can work — I had some great examples of it where I was working. My heart said it would work and I didn't want to hear that he didn't want it. No matter how much fun we had, no matter how hot the chemistry was, he said no relationship, just keep it casual.

It took four times of going back before I could see it wasn't just that. He eventually shared with me other reasons why it wouldn't work for him. In our last encounter in 2022, I saw something new in him, something I had not seen before and that surprised me. What I learned surprised me and showed me that we weren't in fact the match I thought we were. Finally, I could let go. Again, I learned lessons, so no regrets.

Don't be afraid to make mistakes. It is how we learn.

I'm telling you about both of these encounters for example's sake, but of course, there was more nuance to every situation.

What is important is — you learn each time you date someone.

Maybe the lesson won't be clear at the moment of the breakup. Sometimes, fear, shame or doubt that can come during pre-breakup and cloud your thinking. But you can always find a lesson to learn from.

What is also true is that if you don't put yourself out there, you might not learn, you might not grow and you might not find what you need.

It's hard to fail but it is harder to get to what you truly want without these lessons or without trying.

Kayce Interview Part 2

Next you'll read my second interview with Kayce who you met in Chapter 8 on grief. She has been my friend for several years. We've been through a lot together including the loss of her son and both of our divorces. She has stood by my side for many years and I'm grateful for her wisdom.

Kelly

Thanks so much for joining me today. Can you give me some background about your marriage, career and kids.

Kayce

I was working in a career in broadcasting. Keith and I were married after dating for two years.

We were married a good seven years before we had children. When my children were still very young, infants… I stepped back from my career to be home with them. Then, eventually I just worked part time for the next 12 years or so.

The marriage had moments where it was wonderful and then other moments where I knew "not to buy green bananas" together, as they say. I just had a feeling we weren't going to go the distance.

And I had that feeling when the children were still quite young. A terrible feeling to have when your children are so young. And you want above anything else to make them happy and to provide a harmonious, full, intact family for them. So I kind of trudged along. And as I said, we had great moments that were wonderful and these would kind of ebb and flow.

When the kids were in middle school, the marriage just imploded. Around 2011, the marriage was irreparably damaged. As much as I wanted to hang in there for the kids, there comes that moment where you've got to put the oxygen mask on yourself first, right?

And that moment came and it took everything in me to do it. But we could not live together any longer.

After that, I knew I wasn't going to be receiving financial support for the rest of my life and would have to go back to work full time. So, I started training in a new career.

I took classes in healthcare administration and became certified in a whole new line of work, something that was more secure, pretty much a 9-to-5 position allowing me to be home at night with the kids.

So I got very involved with that training, and in a way, it was a lifeline. I had to drive about an hour to class two nights a week. And I remember that drive was a happy one even though I was kind of going backwards, I had a degree, had already had a career).

I was starting from the bottom in a whole new career. It was a challenge. I was taking control of the situation and boy, when you finally take control of a situation, that goes a long way toward your peace of mind.

After completing that course, I got a job and that has been one of the best decisions I've ever made — to go into that field. It has given me security, it's given me wonderful benefits as a single person and it's something I can age into. So, it was a very good move.

Kelly

When you say you were happy that you were doing that — was that hope floating up?

Kayce

Yes. Because when the marriage first fell apart those first few months, you're kind of at odds, you don't know what the future holds. You don't know what's next.

I once read that a lot of women going through divorce have this fear of almost becoming bag ladies. It's some strange fear that a lot of women have, who have maybe been relying on the husband's income. They have this real fear of it going very badly for them.

So, because I made that career move, I didn't have that fear. I knew I was going to be OK.

So yeah, it was a hopeful thing. And again, just that control, charting my own course. If I take this class and pass this test, I will get a job. A plus B equals C.

Kelly

And then there was D for dating. I couldn't help myself.

Kayce

So, I did not date for four years. Part of that was, I think some men and women, if you are put through the mill of a divorce, I think there's a natural tendency for some people to be off the grid. No desire.

I actually struggled thinking, "Am I ever going to want to have a man in my life again?"

I mean, I actually thought, "Am I just going to do the lone wolf thing for the rest of my days?"

I was so soured on relationships and men in general. I hate to say it, but I had no desire. That, plus I was so involved with this new job. I had to learn a whole new industry.

I was now going to work every day and I wanted to be home with the kids. The kids were middle schoolers. They weren't teenagers yet. It was already such an adjustment with their father having moved out and me working full time, I couldn't imagine adding to that.

Kelly
I think it's amazing that you waited four years. I think I waited four weeks.

Kayce
It's a different situation, right?

Kelly
Yeah, my kids were grown.

Kayce
Really what got me dating was my boss. After working with her for a few years, I was at her desk one day just talking about work stuff.

She kind of sat back and looked at me.

She said, "Let me ask you something. Are you dating? You getting out there?"

And I said, "Oh, God, no, no, no, maybe someday."

Her kids had just left for college and I think it was on her mind. She said, "You know, your kids aren't going to be home forever. And you need to start thinking about what's next for you."

I said, "No, you're right. No, I know."

She said, "I'm gonna put up a profile for you if you don't do it."

I said, "Give me six months. Give me till the first of the year."

She said OK. Six months came and went. She forgot about it and then about eight months in, I was at her desk again.

She said, "Hey, it's been more than six months."

I said OK, I'll do it. I think I wanted to drop a little weight. I think I dropped about five pounds to feel a little more sassy, you know.

Kelly
Yeah.

Kayce

When you fill out that [profile] thing, I think back then it was Match, and when you hit that button to post for the first time, that feeling of vulnerability! I think every woman will remember that, when you put your soul out there for the first time. Boom.

Oh my gosh, I just felt like I had no skin all of a sudden.

Kelly
Your insides, your guts are exposed. And I was with <u>you</u> when I first did my profile.

Kayce
Yeah. Right.

Right away though, it started to be fun. It all worked out. The kids were old enough by then and I had no problem going out a couple of nights a week.

But right away I was kind of struck by how much fun I had.

Kelly

The next few questions are about some of the mistakes you made in the beginning and some of the things you did right. You can do whichever one you want first.

Kayce

Some of the mistakes may not be uncommon, if you've been married a long time, and now all of a sudden, you start dating. You may be of a certain age and you're somewhat naive.

I probably wasn't as discerning as I should have been. The more you date, I think the more you can spot, OK, that's not a long hauler. That's two or three dates. We're done.

I think when you're new at it, you kind of hang in there with certain folks that you have some interest in, despite seeing a few red flags.

Kelly

You don't see the red flags, which is what we're going to talk about.

Kayce

I kind of admire those women who are like, "Oh, if he does x, y, z, I'm out."

They've got their standards that are deal breakers. And they're quick to cut.

I once went out with this guy who was an attractive, intelligent guy, he was 5'10" or 5'11".

And he said he once went out with somebody who said, "I thought you were six feet. I'm not interested."

Some standards are a little too much, but I think there's something to be said for seeing red flags. Having the.... I don't know what the word is. Is it maturity? Is it willpower?

I don't know what it is. But to be able to decide to not put any more energy into this, instead of letting things limp along.

Kelly
Well, I do think that definitely needs to be covered — dating does take a lot of energy. It takes a lot of time and these are two of our most precious resources.

If you're not ready to invest in both of those things, then don't do it. Because if you want to be successful, you need to be willing to invest.

It also means you need to be really smart about it, which I think was one of my mistakes. I've wasted my own time going out with people that I didn't have a great feeling about. I'm also the type of person to think, …'but he is nice and I'm nice and so maybe it'll work.' Ugh.

What are the things you did right? Oh and I think waiting was good for you.

Kayce
Right. I think that probably the best thing I did was focus on the new career and the kids. I think that was a really really good thing to do.

I think when I finally did start dating the time was right. But then I would go on and off the dating apps. I would be on for two or three months and then go off for six months or so.

Kelly
Yeah, taking a break from it. I forgot that. Yeah, I think that is the

right thing to do. Like when I have company in town, I just hit snooze on the app. And I focus on who's here and not try to talk to guys.

Kayce
Because it's such a distraction, right? But that can also be a good thing.

Kelly
You were good to give me advice about safety. If you're going someplace and you aren't sure how public it will be or how safe it might be, then you need to share the person's name and phone number if you have it with a friend or family member.

Kayce
Yeah, I had one kind of scary experience, and after that, I made sure to let someone know where I was going. Just say, "Hey, I'm going out and his name is so and so. Here's his number."

Even if you don't have the number and you're just communicating through the app, just say to a friend, "I'm meeting Mike tonight at this local restaurant."

Kelly
Let's talk about when you shared that Maya Angelou quote with me. I was telling you about what Sam said, "I'm an asshole. I'm broke and I'm a male chauvinist."

Kayce
I remember. It was a perfect fit for that quote, because I know the quote from Oprah actually. When I was a stay at home mom, I'd watch Oprah – have her on in the kitchen. So I just knew it. So there we were at the bar that night, and you said, I met this guy, blah, blah, blah. And I said…

Kelly
Believe him.

Kayce
I was like, there it is.

This is a perfect example: I had to talk to you quickly, I thought. She's gonna go out with him for another month.

So it just was the perfect quote. I don't know if I have my own story like that.

I do remember I went out with a man for about seven or eight months. And on one of the first dates he said to me, "I gotta tell you, all men are pigs."

Hahaha. I thought, huh?

Well, first of all, I disagree with that. And secondly, I wouldn't imagine a man who demonstrates that behavior admitting such a thing.

And then later on I got this sense. I think he's been piggish at times during this relationship. I don't think he'd be such a good guy.

Luckily, he was not someone I was in love with or wanted a future with. It was not something I wanted to pursue. And it was, again, very early on. I should have given that more credence or thought than I did.

Kelly
This is something you and I have talked about a lot. And so the next question is, what are some red flags you look for?

Kayce
So if somebody has cheated before, that's a red flag.

Kelly

And if they're open about it, and they talk about it and they say they've learned from it. How do you feel about that? Yeah, it's happened to me twice now. And I couldn't do it.

Kayce

That can be a red flag. I'm not saying every time, I mean, I could see if someone's in a bad marriage. But that's subjective, there are two sides to every marriage. Maybe they should have left the marriage before they did. But infidelity is the kind of behavior that does tend to repeat, so I would be leery. I would definitely be leery.

Other red flags are mixed signals. You know, when you're not quite sure where things stand. I thought he would have called today or texted me.

Oh, and then there is breadcrumbing. (Breadcrumbing is the act of sending out flirtatious, but non-committal social signals (i.e. "breadcrumbs") in order to lure a romantic partner in without expending much effort.)

Once you have to start rationalizing like he's been busy, or he's doing this or that, and I know he had a work thing... You know, how we all do that!

Kelly

I've seen a couple of posts online today. I'm in the Facebook group about dating. It's only women and they talk pretty bluntly. And they were saying, since COVID, there seems to have been an increase in men saying they want a relationship, but then they're trying to have sex on the first date, and I've definitely experienced that.

Kayce

That's another red flag, instantly sexual. You were saying something the other day about certain texts going right to that and that is such low-hanging fruit. To me, that is almost teenage behavior, but I don't want to insult teens. But it's immature.

Kelly

Well, I think if you've been in a bad marriage, and then you weren't having sex for a long time, that can be exciting at first. Yeah, but in reality. I think it was to me, like, oh my god, I'm turning him on. Wow.

But in reality on a first date, that's inappropriate and it's a red flag. I mean, you want there to be chemistry and you want to desire to kiss him. But he shouldn't be asking you to have sex on the first date.

Kayce

Oh, God, no. I'm not saying wait forever, but there's a rhythm to that and if he's jumping the gun, it says something to me.

Kelly

You're gonna feel icky after that.

Kayce

I know that we see other red flags, such as characteristics you may not like.

I remember going out with this guy I liked, but I noticed he would look at every woman, not with that up and down thing, but he would just look at her face. He would just look at her.

I would think, "What are you doing? Do you not realize you're doing that? You're on a date!!"

That relationship didn't go anywhere, but I shouldn't have hung in there as long as I did.

Kelly
No, I could not live with that.

There are two things that have stuck out to me that usually prove to be true.

If somebody complains about their alimony or their divorce or how it went down. Are they still mad and are they gonna stay mad? They have some work to do.

And then the other thing is can he trust women if his wife cheated? I mean, this goes both ways. I've talked to men about it a lot too. But if the spouse cheated, and I'm talking about me too, you really have to try to figure out whether they're over that or not. Because I think that's an energy thing.

Kayce
Agree.

Kelly
Yeah. And the thing I learned recently is this thing called "love bombing." And it may not even be sexual, but love bombing is absolutely a red flag.

When someone says, "Oh my God, you're so special. There isn't anybody like you! You are so amazing. [without knowing all that much about you.]"

And they say, "tell me your life story."

I fell for it twice. Like I really fell for it. Twice!

I've wanted an immediate and undeniable connection because I am so ready to give my love. I just went "OK, here it is."

I had never heard that term and my friend told me, "Well, he was love bombing you.

I said, "What are you talking about?"

She said, "He didn't call you for four days and then he realized he's gonna see you this weekend. So he starts sending you texts and saying 'I can't wait to see you.' He sees you and then boom, he goes dark. And then when he wants to see you, he starts love bombing again."

And then I had a first date and this guy said, "You're a unicorn. You're amazing. I've been looking for you. Where have you been my whole life?"

Kayce
On a first date? Oh my God. Are you serious?

Kelly
Yeah. And then we had a second date and then he ghosts me.

Turns out, he had been drinking before our first date. I didn't know, but then the second date, he said he was hungover. I think he got drunk and he totally love bombed me and then the next day, he was kind of…

Kayce
Almost like a cold fish.

Kelly
Yes! He was totally different.

So there is another red flag — drunk on the first date — not good.

Kayce

I do prefer going for a drink over coffee. I think that is because of nerves.

I always get so nervous before a first date. My heart would be pounding. I can't imagine going for coffee. It's a little too sterile. It's a little too job interviewee.

I do suggest you talk on the phone before the first date.

Kelly

Yeah, I mean, there's been times where I thought 'no way' after the first phone call.

Kayce

You can hit it off texting. There's going to be witty banter, the whole deal, and then you meet them and it's like, oh boy, not interested. So you've got to talk on the phone. Gotta at least have one conversation.

Kelly

I've had a few guys ask to FaceTime. I think they want to see what I look like, which is OK I think.

Kayce

Smart.

Kelly

If they won't FaceTime or they won't talk on the phone. I guess that's probably a red flag.

Kayce

Yes. Yes.

Kelly

OK, I've saved the best for last. You walked with me through my relationship with Blake, who was really my first real crush or love after the divorce. He told me and I didn't listen, that he didn't want a long-distance relationship. I just ignored it and just kept pushing through.

Kayce

You're right. He did say that right away. I remember you telling me that right after you went up there the first time.

Kelly

I think I was kind of love bombing him in a way by trying to change his mind through expressing my feelings. It was about how he made me feel. I thought, "Oh my god, this is it."

Kayce

Awesome. Yeah, this is amazing.

Kelly

I hadn't had that feeling in a very <u>long</u> time and wanted to know when we were gonna see each other again.

He said, "I didn't come to Nashville thinking I'm gonna find a girl and have a long-distance relationship."

I said, "No, I didn't go out with you thinking of a long-distance relationship either, but you're here. And we've hit it off. We have all this good stuff in common."

Kayce

You had a connection.

Kelly

Yes, a connection. And I wanted to follow through on it and he said we can follow through on it, we just have to keep it casual. And I was the one who said, "I'll come up and see you."

So we dated for a few months and had I listened from the beginning, I would have saved my time and energy.

Kayce
Yeah. I think that your story is actually pretty important because he *was* telling you. It's a perfect example of how we have to listen to what people are saying.

Don't be so busy trying to impress them. Think about you. Do you like them? Do you want them? Do you enjoy them?

Kelly
That is awesome.

And I don't want to be a woman 20 years later who is still trying to figure it out, with nobody left to swipe right or left on, you know?

Next question. What feeds your soul?

Kayce
That's where I am fortunate, in that I did eventually meet someone. His name is Brad and he's brought much joy to my life.

I also am the kind of person who needs to refuel — a little bit of an introvert.

I work full time. I'm up early and right onto the computer to start my workday. I manage a team, so Monday through Friday is bananas.

Saturday mornings I try to keep as this little personal time.

It's my time to catch up on reading. Time to get lost in a novel or learn something, time to nurture some intellectual curiosity.

Kelly
I was gonna say it sounds like intellect, like that's nurturing and that feeds your soul. And also your time with Brad.

OK, if you get sad, what do you do to self soothe?

Kayce
I am kind of a comedy nerd. I love comedy. I like stand-up comics. I like watching comedies. I like SNL, the late-night comedians. That has gotten me through… and a lot of music.

I've said music, comedy and friends are what have gotten me through my darkest days.

Music is a biggie for me. It has been since I was a kid.

Time with friends has gotten harder. You've moved away, other friends have left the area. COVID put a real wrench in the whole hanging out with friends thing, it hasn't gotten back to where it was quite yet.

Kelly
It'll be interesting to see who is still around and how people have made a lot of changes.

Kayce
Yeah, interesting, but that's soul feeding.

Kelly
What are you hopeful for?

Kayce
It's interesting, when my ex-husband and I first split and I had to

make that call to my parents... you know — that call everyone has to make when their marriage ends... You feel like a failure.

I called my parents. I told them and my mother said,

"The best is yet to come."

And I thought, wow. I want to believe that but here I am, this long marriage is ending and these two beautiful kids' lives are going to be upended....

I get emotional even now. It was a heartbreaking time. I thought, "how can the best be yet to come?"

But I realized, she's talking just to me, about MY happiness. And I just had to choose to believe her.

I used to think, "Is that special guy out there, the one with whom I'll spend this next chapter?"

"I don't know what he's doing right now. But I know he's out there somewhere."

So to have found someone now, and see what my mother predicted coming true, is pretty extraordinary.

But she gave me hope. I just had to choose to believe it. The best was yet to come.

Kelly
Any last advice for people going through a big change?

Kayce
You cannot be paralyzed by fear. You have to face whatever you're afraid of.

"Oh, I'm too old to get back out there."

"I don't look the way I want to look."

You have to face whatever or wherever it comes from; fear or feelings of inadequacy.

You've got to stare that thing down and beat it. Beat that with a stick!

> Gotta live life. Life rewards action. There's joy to be experienced. You've got to put yourself out there.

I think the biggest thing is fear stops a lot of people. You've got to be vulnerable.

There's a Brené Brown quote about how staying vulnerable is a risk we take if we want to experience connection.

Take that risk by hitting that button to post your dating profile even when you're 50 years old and have not been on a date in 30 years!

That is a risk you've got to take in order to experience whatever connections are out there to be made.

So yeah, good advice. Do not fear.

Empowerment Practice 10: Clarify Your Behavior Cycles

I've suggested in Chapter 2 that you create a resume, make a list of your qualities and to do this, you need to make time for reflection. But you also need to look at yourself within the relationships you have had. From parents to siblings, from dating to marriage, friendships to breakups, you need to look for repeated behavior.

Can you identify cycles in your own behavior? Remember my story about Sam? Let's pretend you are him for a minute. If you were going to warn someone on a first date about your bad traits or habits, what would they be?

Go for it. Write it down. No one has to see it unless you want. There might be some shame there and there might be some pride. Whatever you see, write it down.

YOU ARE HUMAN! You have made mistakes. We all do. Take a look at yourself deep within, see and name the repeated behaviors and then forgive yourself.

Start by answering these questions and see if they reveal repeated behaviors:

1. Within your nuclear family, as a child, how did you act out within your parental relationships?
    Example: I was constantly needing attention from my father.

2. If you have siblings, how did you interact within those relationships in the early years?

Example: I was resentful of my older sister's overprotective nature.

3. While dating at a young age, what behaviors do you remember?
    Example: I tended to be very serious too quickly.

4. Within your early friendships, how did your relationships emerge and evolve?
    Example: I wanted to be friends with more popular people and was eager for their attention. I became a doormat.

5. Within a marriage or partnership, how did you handle conflict?
    Example: I never backed down in a fight and fully believed I was right.

Now, review all these patterns and try to define where you can take responsibility. This is when you begin to heal and begin to forgive yourself. No matter how bright your future might be, if you are not looking within and looking to address patterns, you are in danger of repeating destructive behavior.

Lastly, I'd like you to list five positive behaviors that you can aspire to live out starting today. Think what you want reflected back to you whether it is from friends, family, or a partner.

Write them in present tense. Consider placing this list on a Post-it note somewhere you see it every day. Bathroom mirrors and car dashboards work great.

For example:

1. I am going to smile at each person I pass each day because a smile is contagious.
2. I will be honest with family and friends about my feelings when I've had a bad day.
3. I will share what attributes I love about my friends and family so they feel my love.

SYMBOLS ARE POWERFUL BECAUSE THEY ARE THE
VISIBLE SIGNS OF INVISIBLE REALITIES." – SAINT
AUGUSTINE

_____

CHAPTER 11:
PERSPECTIVE AND SIGNS

How can you keep your head up and search for happiness without denying yourself the need to feel what you need to feel? This is a real question and there is not an easy answer.

Even when it hurt like hell, I continued to search for joy. I know this may sounds over simplified. It's not.

Let's just take the physical aspect of this idea.

Standing outside, you look down, you see your feet and a circumference of say, 4 feet around you and a 180-degree span. You begin to walk down a path in the woods. It is important to look down and watch where your feet are going and to avoid obstacles such as tree roots, rocks, puddles and possibly holes in the ground.

Now you begin to walk down the path and you look up. You look side to side, you can turn your head 360 degrees just with a few steps. You have increased your perspective. You can now see a thorny branch sticking out. You can see the flowers that are blooming along the path. You can see a bench up ahead where you can rest.

Now, let's look up — way up into the sky. You see a tree branch with a bird's nest and a mother bird flying to find food for her baby birds. You see a plane traveling to an unknown place. You see clouds in motion on their way across the country.

There is no limit to what you can see. Right?

Let's take a look at each of these views or perspectives in a relationship sense.

The Safe Place

When someone is not letting the world in or not putting themselves out in the world, this is the "head down" phase. Many of us, especially in times of pain or sorrow, go within ourselves, our homes, or our relationships. If we isolate ourselves, it can be dangerous because when we have our head down, it is almost impossible to find our way out.

When I was in this place, I stopped going to church where I had been very involved. I started running by myself instead of with a group or a friend. I was not telling anyone how unhappy I was. I was ashamed that my world was so screwed up. I was just surviving because holding together my broken heart took all the energy I had. I had hardly anything to give — or so I thought.

Yes, there is a time and place in all of our lives to feel like and live like this. It's called self-preservation and we all have instincts that fire and tell us to go to a safe place.

There is nothing wrong with you if you find yourself here. It is just a season of life where your soul is preparing for the next steps.

The Horizon

Once you begin to feel the need to escape this place of isolation, your heart and mind are showing you that you are stuck in a place where you cannot grow. You begin to feel an overwhelming urge to scan the horizon and look for a place to go, to be, to breathe.

I believe this means you have grown stronger. Your soul is telling you it's time.

I felt this when I finally realized how trapped I'd felt and how long I'd felt that way. I'd been fighting so hard to save my marriage, I had completely lost myself. But once this reality became apparent, I needed to scan the horizon. I needed to reconnect with my friends and family. I needed their support.

I began to seek out friends I believed would see the broken me, hold me up and help me find the next steps. God, I don't know what I would have done without their vision of who I was and who I could be. They could see my strength, my resilience and my drive even when I had forgotten that innate part of me.

"One day at a time," they would say.

"One minute at a time," I thought.

The mentality had already been something I practiced. When training for a half-marathon with my daughter, we used interval training. I told her what I said to myself to keep pushing through in the later miles. I said, "I can do anything for one minute."

Now I needed to apply that resiliency to getting myself unstuck.

You too, with or without friends, have the ability to pull out of the tough places, out of your hole, out of your own head.

> Your heart can heal and the sooner you believe that,
> the sooner it will begin to happen.

It likely will be a long path to walk down to find peace and wholeness, much less joy. But it is a path worth traveling because it is such a beautiful place at the end of this path. This place is called peace.

Seeing the Signs

My looking up, my first glimpse of the horizon, began on Dec. 9, 2017, just weeks after my marriage's true darkness reared its ugly head. Garth was visiting and telling my in-laws about our split.

I love them so much and it devastated me to know how this was going to affect them. I feared how I might lose them, but I had no control over the situation.

Dan, a best friend to both Garth and me, called to check on me. He comforted me and he suggested that I needed a distraction.

"Why don't you finally watch that movie I've been begging you to watch? This is the perfect time," said Dan.

I asked him to remind me what the movie was. It was _The Way_ and I found it on Amazon Prime. This was a movie about hiking the Camino de Santiago in Spain, an ancient pilgrimage that hundreds of thousands of people walk each year. (If you watch this movie, just go ahead and buy it because you WILL want to watch it again.)

I started watching the movie and was thinking, "There is no way I can do the Camino — look at all those beds in the hostel."

I am a terrible sleeper and that looked like torture. And it's a 500-mile walk!

Then Garth called, shared with me that his parents had been emotional, but were "fine" and that they were all exhausted and going to bed. Fine? Well, I wasn't fine. How could they be fine?

Trying to keep my mind from spiraling to a dark place, I restarted the movie and 30 minutes later, Dan called to check on me. I told him my thoughts on those hostels and he just laughed.

"Just give it a chance, Kel," he said. "I think you need this."

So instead of watching the movie, I asked him to share with me what a day on the Camino is like. We ended up talking until 1:45 a.m. I actually fell asleep listening to him sharing about his experience and how beautiful it had been.

"It saved me," he said.

I awoke at 5 a.m. — kind of pissed off that I couldn't sleep. I needed to sleep badly as I'd been basically an insomniac for six weeks.

I went downstairs, pushed the Keurig button and poured the creamer into the coffee, just like hundreds of other days.

Then I decided to watch the movie.

Dan was right.

The movie showed how transformative the Camino can be for a person who has experienced great loss. It wasn't what I was expecting and by the end of the movie, I had tears running down my face.

"I have to talk to Crystal," I said out loud to no one. "This is like what she did when she went to her retreat abroad."

I stand up and walk across the room to turn off the television and my cell phone rings. It's Crystal.

Ten seconds after I thought of her, she is calling.

I answered laughing and crying all at the same time.

"You are not going to believe this," I said. "I literally just said out loud that I needed to talk to you."

I caught her up on everything that had happened, my talk with Dan and the movie.

"God is so good!" she said. "I'm in town for a wedding shower so let's get together today."

We made a plan to meet that afternoon and I went about my day, got in my run and went to the office.

I arrived early and I had the place to myself. I picked up my devotional _Jesus Calling_ by Sarah Young and opened it to the day. I had not picked up this book in a long time and it surprised me that I grabbed it.

I began to read and I began to cry.

"Be willing to go out on a limb with Me. If that is where I am leading you, it is the safest place to be. Your desire to live a risk-free life is a form of unbelief. Your longing to live close to Me is at odds with your attempts to minimize risk. You are approaching a crossroads in your journey. In order to follow Me wholeheartedly, you must relinquish your tendency to play it safe.

Let Me lead you step by step through this day. If your primary focus is on Me, you can walk along perilous paths without being afraid. Eventually, you will learn to relax and enjoy the adventure of our journey together. As *long as you stay close to Me, My sovereign Presence protects you wherever you go."*

RELATED SCRIPTURE:

Psalm 23:4 (NLT)

4 Even when I walk

   through the darkest valley,

I will not be afraid,

   for you are close beside me.

Your rod and your staff

   protect and comfort me.

I felt like this was a sign and I knew I was going to go walk the Camino.

Crystal and I got together that afternoon and, in what I considered to be another sign, she basically repeated words to me that Dan had been saying the night before. They both urged me to see that I deserve better. The healthy thing to do was to move on and going to Spain would be a great start.

I laughed and cried. With friends like these, I knew I could do it.

What you look for is what you see

The first person I met on the Camino was Brandi, whom you heard from in Chapter 1. We met the night we arrived in Bayonne, France.

A few days later, as we were walking to Zubiri, Brandi saw a rock shaped like a heart and picked it up. I was so excited because I had never seen a heart rock before and I said so.

She shared that she believed I probably had walked right over them, I just hadn't been looking for it. Hmmmm, I thought. There was a little spark that lit when she said it.

Later on down the path, we saw a puddle in the shape of a perfect heart.

"See!" she says excitedly. *"If you look for it, you see it."*

I walked along taking that statement to a deeper level.

What am I looking for on this hike? What will the pilgrimage show me if I open my eyes and my heart?

My heart was what I needed to heal. I had to focus on my heart.

Brandi Interview Part 2

Let's hear more from Brandi about the topic of signs.

Kelly

Did you start seeing heart rocks before you went on the Camino?

Because, just so you know, I never stopped seeing them after that day with you and I see them everywhere I go. I have jars of them. I like to give them to people.

The rocks became a metaphor for me. It was probably my first realization of manifestation or initiation meaning that if I'm looking for something, I will find it.

If I'm looking for pain and that's all I think about, I'm gonna have more pain. If I'm looking for love I'm gonna find love. If I'm looking for a heart rock, I'm gonna find a heart rock. A heart leaf. A heart pond.

And to me, it's a metaphor for what I want.

Brandi

For me, it's double sided. Because the first night when we stayed in Bayonne, I went to the hotel after our dinner and I'm going to charge my phone. And it didn't charge.

And everything flashed through my head.

I was thinking, "How am I supposed to call my family? How am I supposed to take pictures? How am I going to post things on social media? How will I wake up in the morning to catch the bus?"

Everything.

Then I realized that my mother had given me an extra charger.

I took it out because I wanted to try to charge it and the name of this brand on this charger was Trust. That was the first message that I got.

I was like, I'm lying here. I know I'm going to be here for three weeks or so. What will be the worst thing if I wake up too late? So that first message was trust.

And I had to trust. I had to trust whatever was going to happen was supposed to happen. And just to let go of my need to try to control everything.

I know that there is a source that is far greater than me. For me, it's not about religion. It's a universal intelligence.

Kelly
Universal Intelligence. I like Universal Intelligence. That's cool.

Brandi
Yeah, so that was my first message, trust. And that's why I had to go on the Camino by myself. Because, for me, it was a spiritual journey. I had to trust the universe.

And then when I bought the Camino shell.[7] I saw the heart-shaped hole and the heart was starting to appear everywhere. So trust and

---

[7] Camino pilgrims carry a scallop shell tied to their backpacks so they can identify each other. It also represents the journey and is a symbolic item to bring home to remember the journey.

love was the message for me the whole journey. And it's still the same.

Seeing the rocks? It wasn't like I was looking for them. It was more like I got to see them when I was not expecting them to show up.

But then I thought about the law of attraction. I can visualize something and I can get it. And that was what I did.

I think it was after you and I separated on the trail.

I said, 'I'm going to try and see if the law of attraction works."

OK, I decided what would be the first thing that I asked for from the universe. I said I wanted an apple as we were walking.

Later that day, we found this albergue[8] and we were sitting outside having dinner at night.

A woman came to our table and said, 'You know what? I went to the store and I found a perfect big apple but I can only eat half of it because it's so big. Is there any one of you who wants this apple?"

I said yep and that was the same day. And I thought, "Oh, it worked!"

And then the second time I said, "OK universe, give me a feather. How hard can it be?"

---

[8] Albergue is a hostel that is for pilgrims hiking the camino. You must have pilgrim credentials to stay at the facility.

So later that night, we went to a pilgrim mass and outside the church where we were standing, there was this feather just in front of me circling in the air. And that was like, "Ok, got it."

And the third thing that I asked for, I needed to figure out something that will be really hard, you know? And I was like, "Yep, I want a heart-shaped cloud. Yep, that is what I want."

I was looking and I didn't see any. And then the last day I had with my fellow pilgrim, Victoria, we were in a small fishing village near Santiago de Compostela.

We were having lunch and all of a sudden we heard a cannon shot! You know, where they have a big boom.

And I was like what's that? The waiter told us that they celebrated the fishermen that day with this cannon.

And I looked up in the sky, the cannon made a heart-shaped cloud.

I was like, "You're kidding me! It's the grand finale!"

It's like we get heard. And I thought, "You can't make this up."

It's Universal Intelligence with us all of the way. They give whatever it is. They hear us. They give us what we need. All the time. We just need to ask for it.

Crystal Interview Part 2

Dreams and Spiritual Experiences

Now I'd like to share more from Crystal. As you'll recall, when she was in the process of healing and recovering from her tough divorce, she was also in grad school. While doing research, she learned how to see guidance from the universe, She also took a sabbatical spiritual journey to the holy Scottish Isle of Iona. She had a special dream about the trip and then she had an experience there that changed her perspective.

Kelly

When did you start believing in signs?

Crystal

I think that all women, even as little girls, are intuitive. We see things and we understand those things are not random. There is meaning to life. All of life.

Then, at some point, we're taught to distrust our intuitive knowing and more than that, we are taught not to trust feminine power. It feels very threatening to the world and thus very threatening to us.

That is what happened to me. I remember having vivid dreams when I was around five years old. The next day, I would see something that made me believe my dreams were real. My parents were uncomfortable when I told them these things. So I stopped telling them. Then I stopped noticing. I didn't trust myself. I thought I had a wild imagination. And that somehow was a bad thing in my world.

Kelly

How has this evolved for you?

Crystal

In 2010, after learning for the first time that James was cheating, I told my therapist, "I think I always knew." I wanted to explore this inner knowing I had dismissed as a young girl. Because I was in divinity school, I wanted to think about it theologically as well. She recommended I see Psychic Frank, an intuitive healer.

I made an appointment to see him. I told him I was studying theology and am wondering about what Macrina Weidacher calls "the inner I AM," an inner wisdom in each of us that is from God.

Psychic Frank is one of the most precious and gentle souls I've ever known. I loved and trusted him immediately.

We were having this conversation, kind of academically, and then he said, "I can see you are surrounded by a lot of male energy in your life here."

I told him that was true, four sons, husband, father, brother, nephews, etc...

He said, "In the other realm, on the other side of the veil, you are surrounded by female energy. There's a long line of women holding you up. They want you to know that they had to make certain choices in their lives, but you don't have to make the same choices. You have a different path."

He called them "the grandmothers" and said they want me to know that I have power to make some changes in my life.

Then he said, "They all have feathers now. So this is to be the sign that you are on the new path. Feathers. When you see feathers, know that they are with you, that you are not alone. And say thank you."

So, just like with the heart rocks that were shown to you and that you now see often, feathers are everywhere for me. I began to learn all the kinds of feathers. Blue jay and hawk feathers are my favorites.

And so anyway, feathers were the first sign. I started collecting stones because Iona was full of stones. I had always collected shells but I began to see all these things as gifts from my inner self or soul to my physical self.

Kelly
Say more about how this has helped you.

Crystal
These signs helped me trust myself, my inner wisdom.

I started talking about signs and symbols to other people. I introduced it into my work through meditation and visualization practices. It was very effective.

I learned that when I'm attending to my soul — somebody else's soul responds — and being a spiritual leader is just that — leading others toward their own path of soul care and transformation.

Kelly
You have done a lot around dreams in your work. Tell me about your dream and Iona.

Crystal
I think at that time I had this wild dream about enlightenment.

This is the part of the dream I remember. I had a red kayak and I went a little way over the island and then stopped. There were people at each stop who told me when I could go on to the next stop.

At each stop, they'd say, "Just stay here and teach this."

And I said, "Teach what?"

They never gave the lesson. Only saying, "Teach this to yourself."

Over and over again, I was a nomad at the top of the world and there's nothing there.

I finally understood the lesson which was to accept that — wherever I go, there I am.

And this too — people will show up for you.

Picking up the missing pieces myself became fun.

Kelly
Iona sounds like it was transformational.

Crystal
It's a jaunt to get to Iona. I flew to Glasgow and spent a whole day there.

I was by myself because I had decided I was not going to make friends, which is just the funniest thing. I didn't want to meet anybody. So I spent that whole day in a Glasgow cemetery.

After Glasgow, I got on a train to Oban. I spent the night then took a ferry to Mull. There's a bus that takes you across Mull to another ferry.

It takes about two days.

While waiting on the ferry on the far side of the Isle of Mull, I'm looking toward Iona. And I felt like Iona was my mother.

"Why am I here?" I said.

And she said, "Well, I invited you here of course."

Iona is small. I could walk the whole island in a day. There were marshy areas, beaches, pastures and a little village. There was a high area with a well dedicated to St. Brigid. It is a holy place and there are many holy places on the island.

There's a goddess whose statues are found all through Wales, Ireland and Scotland. She's called the Sheelah na gig.

The statue is a woman with her legs spread, her vulva is like right in your face. She's found everywhere that feels holy. There's one on Iona in the ruins of the old convent destroyed by the Vikings thousands of years ago.

So I was going to see her in the ruins and I felt into my pocket and there was a movie ticket. This ticket was from the last night I was with James. That *Superman* movie ticket represented my old life.

And so I decided to give Sheelah na gig the ticket. I put it in the rocks around her statue and then I turned around and walked down the hill and in my head I heard her yell at me.

"Hey, come back."

She was mad. Then I got mad.

I got the feeling she was saying, "I don't want him. You take him."

And I said, "No, I will not. You take him."

And she said, "Are you sure?"

And I said, "I am sure. It's hard. I'm trying. I came to Iona to let him go, to get rid of him. You take him!"

"I've been trying to give him up since all this went down, but he keeps coming back."

She said, "He doesn't come back — you keep taking him back."

I knew then she was right. In more traditional Christian imagery, it was like I was laying this at the cross for Jesus to keep. And then I turned around and picked it back up. That realization was an awesome gift to help me move forward.

There is another holy place in Iona — it's a cave on the western shore of the isle. It was like going back into the mother's womb, and emerging and being born again. That was super powerful.

I took pictures of the cave and I made a book months later. When I had to go to depositions and advocate for myself, my book was full of these pictures combined with my own thoughts and prayers, or poems that reminded me I'm strong.

It helped me to remember that all of this legal process that's going on around me in this deposition, this divorce trauma, is not even part of my world. It's temporary.

Kelly
Any advice for people going through a change? And with perspective?

Crystal

We walk by faith and not by sight so you have
to trust people who can see beyond the horizon
a little bit further than you can.

Make a nest for yourself. This was great advice from my friend.

When I mentioned my cabin on the mountain to her, she said get comfortable. I bought the nicest sheets I could find and big comfy pillows.

Every hotel room in Scotland had these little electric kettles. To remind myself of that holy time, I bought one of those. I set up a little tea station in my room. I had all my magic and all my "woo woo"[9] stuff around me.

That was an important thing to me because of this cycle that began in 2010. And continues to today.

Sometimes I would have to just leave work in the middle of the day and say I'll be back in an hour. I'd have to go home and get curled up in my bed. I just had to have that nest. The rest of the house was not anything special, but the bedroom was my sanctuary.

---

[9] **woo woo** - A person readily accepting supernatural, paranormal, occult, or pseudoscientific phenomena, or emotion-based beliefs and explanations.

Empowerment Practice 11: Walking Meditation for Perspective

I want to take you back to the beginning of the chapter when I had you visualize walking down a path. We are going to take a walk.

If at all possible, the first part of this exercise should be done outside on a flat safe area preferably a walking path. If that is not possible, the hallway of a building or a gymnasium would work. The second part of the exercise will be done in your workshop or if you can create a nest — that works too!

If you would like to remove distractions because the area is noisy, feel free to use headphones or earbuds. But what I recommend you do is put on white noise or use a sound machine to provide a soothing noise such as running water.

Part 1: Perspective Walk

1. Think about one thing that is holding you back right now. Give it a name of no more than three words and use past tense if possible. For example: "I wasn't confident" or "I was lonely."

    While walking about 100 yards at a casual pace looking down at your feet, repeat those three words slowly. Keep your feet moving and your head down as your perspective. Don't turn your head or look around unless it is necessary for safety. Note what you are seeing as you walk because you will write this down later.

2. If safe, close your eyes and stand still. Safety first though!
    While counting to five, slowly take a big breath in. Now
    breathe it out counting to five. Do this five times. Relax your
    shoulders, your arms, shake out your legs.

3. Now think of something in your life that is positive and
    brings you joy. Name it in three words in present tense. For
    example: "I am growing" or "I love music" or "Talking to
    children"

    Now walk another 100 yards at a casual pace looking ahead
    while repeating your joyful words. This time you may turn
    your head side to side. Take in what you are seeing because
    later I will ask you to write this down.

4. If safe, close your eyes and stand still. While counting to
    five, slowly take in a big breath. Now breathe it out counting
    to five. Do this five times. Relax your shoulders, your arms,
    shake out your legs.

5. Find a place where you can see the sky, preferably not under
    a tree or next to a big building. If you are inside, you will
    close your eyes and use your imagination here.

    Think of something you want in your future life that you
    feel is missing. Name it in a few words and use present
    tense. For example: "I'm in love" or "I'm grateful" or
    "Walking the beach."

    Stand with your feet hip distance apart. Take in a deep

breath raising your arms over your head. Spread your fingers wide and reach for the sky. As you breathe out, lower your arms. If you are inside, close your eyes but still look up and imagine clouds floating overhead and the infinite blue sky.

6. Now very slowly turn in a circle five times or walk in a circle if possible keeping your eyes on the sky and repeating your words. Smile while you are doing this. Feel your body moving, see the infinite sky, imagine a kite flying above or a plane soaring overhead.

    Remember to note what you saw in this perspective.

7. If safe, close your eyes. While counting to five, slowly take a big breath in. Now breathe it out counting to five. Do this five times. Relax your shoulders, your arms, shake out your legs. Smile!

Part 2: Remembrance

Go to a safe place, hopefully your workshop or nest. Bring pen and paper or open a blank document on your computer.

1. Write down your thoughts from Part 1 when your head was down.
    o   How did you feel repeating those words while walking?
    o   What did you see? Did you feel restricted?
    o   How did it feel to breathe afterward?

2. Write down your thoughts from perspective 2 when you could look up and around.

- How did you feel repeating your joyful words? Did you smile?
- What did you see as you looked around? Did you feel more free?
- How did it feel to breathe afterward this time? Was it different?

3. Write down your thoughts from perspective 3 when you were looking up and reaching for the sky.
    - How did you feel repeating your future hopes while looking up?
    - What did you see as you looked up? Did you feel hopeful, free or challenged?
    - How did it feel to breathe afterward? Was it different?

If you ever feel stuck, come back to this exercise. Use it to free your mind and breathe.

"FIRST BEST IS FALLING IN LOVE. SECOND BEST IS BEING IN LOVE. LEAST BEST IS FALLING OUT OF LOVE. BUT ANY OF IT IS BETTER THAN NEVER HAVING BEEN IN LOVE." – MAYA ANGELOU

CHAPTER 12:
LET'S TALK DATING

As we begin the chapter on dating, I first want to say thank you for coming on this ride with me. It's been a process for me to walk through the details of my living, loving and losing, and then growing and gaining.

My friend Kaye said to me that writing this book is me fulfilling the need to use my pain for good. That's a beautiful way to look at the process I've walked through.

Another friend Crystal shared with me a quote by <u>Duke basketball coach, Kara Lawson</u>, from a speech to her team.

"...we all wait in life for things to get easier. I've just got to get through this and life will be easier... It's what we do. We wait for stuff to get easier. It will never get easier.

"What happens is you become someone that handles hard stuff better. So that's a mental shift that has to occur in each of our brains...

"So make yourself a person who handles the hard well. Not someone that's waiting on the easy. Because if you have a meaningful pursuit in life, it will never be easy....

"So don't get discouraged through this time if it's hard. It's supposed to be. And don't wait for it to be easy. And whatever comes at you, you'll be great."

Tough words but oh, so true!

Now, when it comes to dating and your healing process, not everyone is going to want to start at the same time. As you've read in multiple interviews, it is a very personal choice. When you are ready, here is some wisdom I want to pass along.

As scary as it may sound, dating is so much fun!

> But...you must go into it with eyes wide open,
> heart wide open and red flag goggles on.

Dating is making yourself vulnerable, as we learned from Kayce. Dating is a place we can make mistakes, we can get hurt and we can see people at their worst.

And, yes, Coach Lawson, we also want it to get easier.

I have already walked through one of my worst nightmares but I'm hopeful and I'm strong. I'm not waiting for it to get easier because I've already learned how to do the hard stuff.

I handle hard things well now.

And so can you!

All the single women you have met throughout these chapters have agreed on one thing. Did you notice most had read and listened to Brené Brown?

From Brown's perspective, you must be vulnerable. That's where courage starts. I hope that, when you are ready, you are getting into that ring and fighting for what you want.

You will make mistakes. And you need to give yourself grace. Think through the lessons to take from each experience and release it.

You will also have fun and find hope.

> When that someone looks at you like 'that' or you get that 'zing' when they touch your hand, find hope in that.

I could list all the mistakes I've made, but I'm not sure it would help you right now.

What I will share instead is what I learned about myself and dating:

1. I lit up when speaking to someone I was attracted to. Sometimes it sent them running and sometimes it made them come on strong. I wasn't reserving my light for someone who deserved it which I am doing differently going forward. For example, I am more aware of how someone is reacting to my words rather than just answering the question. I am not attempting to impress them but connect with them. Check.

2. Just because I am an open book, and honest to a fault, doesn't mean everyone deserves to hear my story (or wants to). I am now more choosey about where I share my energy. Crystal shared this with me.

3. I fall in and I fall fast. I have a hard time taking it slow once I feel the chemistry is strong. I had to learn I am worth

waiting for and that taking my time not only protects my heart, it reminds me of my worth. Even more importantly, it shows my potential partner my worth. My sister pointed this out to me.

4. No matter how nice a guy is, if the chemistry is not there, it is not there. I dated a super nice guy in Boston one summer and "on paper" he had everything I wanted: authenticity, love of travel, kindness. No real red flags. But I kept dating him for too long and kept hoping the chemistry would eventually show up. It didn't and I hurt him. I had to learn from this to be honest with myself — this isn't about being nice. His time matters too.

5. I learned about the personality types that are good or not good for me. Although this is not a hard and fast rule, it is definitely something to consider. The longest relationship I have had was with Antonio, a passionate Latin man. Early on, he described himself as an extroverted introvert. It turned out to be difficult for me when he had moments or seasons of intense introversion. It was confusing and hard not to feel like I had done something wrong. In fact, it was a trigger, taking me back to my feelings of rejection from my marriage. There was a lack of communication on both sides, but I learned from it that if someone is an introvert, we would need to have very good communication.

6. The one that got away — I learned to trust that they should. Sometimes there is something missing. Sometimes it is simply timing. But going back and revisiting old relationships is frequently a waste of time. I can't force it and I sure can't make them force it either. I learned to let it go

and walk in the other direction. That's where my happiness is!

7. Talk about sex before you have it. When I find a connection, I need to take my time developing a relationship. If I take that time up front, we will know each other better when it is time to address the physical aspects of dating. The more comfortable I am, the more likely it is that an open connection will carry over to the bedroom. Many of us had marriages where sex talk wasn't a thing — now is the time to change that. It might not be easy — but hopefully it will be. Yet, it is too important not to address it up front.

Getting Started - Vroom Vroom

Dating Apps - Between my girlfriends and me, I feel like we've tried them all. There are some that are more appropriate for different age groups and some that have a more casual or serious clientele, but you really just have to decide what you are looking for and perhaps be willing to use some trial and error.

o Paid versions provide a lot more features and give you access to more information. I found it more useful to use the paid version, but I always did it for short periods of time.

o Some apps provide your profile only to people who match your desired mate. In some, other people can see your profile and approach you even if they do not meet the desirable qualities you listed. For example, Match lets people who don't fit the profile you're looking for see your info and Bumble does not. I would get hit up by 70 year olds on Match — not what I wanted! So, Bumble's age filters were a fit for me.

- ○ You can pause the app. If you meet someone, and you want to give it some time for a few days or a week without further distraction, you can pause the app until you want to talk to new people again. This is easier than deleting your account and having to recreate it.
- ○ It is time consuming to communicate with multiple people at a time. It takes energy. When you first get on, it can be overwhelming because you are the new kid on the block and could have lots of suitors. You can use pause for fatigue as well!

Safety - You must think about your safety at all times. Kayce and I touched on this in Chapter 9.

- ○ Please do NOT meet in an isolated location — not even a public park, unless there are people around you. Always meet where there are lots of people nearby. Once I was asked to go for a run on a first date. At first that sounded fun, but then I thought, would I want my daughter doing that? Hell no!
- ○ When you are going on a date, especially a first date, let a friend know who you are going out with, where and what time. Send a picture of the date to your friend.
- ○ There are location sharing options on both iPhones and Androids. Find someone you trust who won't be checking on you or spying out of nosiness. If something happens, they will know where you are. I've even dropped this information on my date so the person knows.

- If you get uncomfortable, tell the date to back off and why. If you feel unsafe, you do not owe anyone an explanation. You can also just make an excuse to leave.
- Always drive yourself to a first date. You should have your own way home. There are times you may have to walk away from an uncomfortable situation.
- If you are uncomfortable or nervous for your safety, talk to the bartender, a waitress or anyone working in the establishment. You can ask someone to walk you to your car. This is not embarrassing — this is your life. I've done this multiple times.

Define Wants & Needs - It's OK to not know what you want right away. But be clear about what you DON'T want.

- Yes, there are people, men and women, who are looking for only sex. You need to develop questions that cut to the chase if casual sex is not of interest to you. Use those questions to eliminate suitors. Example: *Have you had any relationships since your divorce? What is your longest relationship?*
- Be clear about your intentions. For example, *I am looking for my person. I'm not interested in casual dating — I want a relationship*. Or if the opposite is true, tell them that's what you are looking for. It's not always easy, but I've learned to be extremely clear. I have a vision statement written on a Post-it note that I carry with me as a reminder.
- You are NOT going to change someone. If they are not looking for what you are, move on, no matter how damn good looking they are!
- One thing I knew I did not want to fill my daily life was younger kids. I've raised my three amazing daughters to

adulthood and I'm not prepared to raise someone else's kids. Have you thought of this aspect? It is really important to define this.

- o Life goals and financial expectations matter. If you want someone who matches your financial situation, be clear about it. If you want to travel, be up front. I dated a great guy in Savannah but he later revealed he wanted someone to stay home with him and be a housewife. I am very active, I need to travel and I need a partner who will do that with me.

Excitement - Ladies and Gentlemen, Start your engines! Your ego is going to get a boost (and a deflation) along the way, but let's make sure we're watching out for those red flags.

- o Man, it feels good when you match — enjoy it! Chat and have fun with it. Flirt!
- o You won't match with everyone you like. It happens more often that you don't match. Trust it! "Thank you, next!" says pop star Ariana Grande. (Great song!)
- o People may ask for extra pictures — don't do it. If they send you unsolicited inappropriate pictures, block them quickly. Don't be polite. This is a red flag about respecting boundaries.
- o Some people will be untruthful. They may just bend it a little. But if you get a whiff of dishonesty — that is a red flag flying. Move on!
- o There are spammers that act like prince charming. If you are seeing phrasing that is broken English, someone is overly complimentary and their replies don't quite make sense, it

could be a sign that you are being catfished[10]. This is one potential thing to look out for and is not at all to say that person with English as a second language are dangerous. This has happened to me several times. If those pics are too good to be true, they just might be.

Dates - Great first date ideas and ways to meet someone.

- o Having a phone call or FaceTime is a great first date. Less pressure for how you look or how nervous you are. I highly recommend this.
- o Meet for coffee during the day if possible. If you are looking to be casual, this is a good move. I don't recommend dinner for a first date.
- o If you can only meet at night, you can meet for a drink or dessert. But don't have more than one drink even if you are having fun. Drink water before and after the one drink. And never leave your drink alone with your date or a group of people you don't know. Finish it before you walk away or don't drink it when you return.
- o Go bowling or play pool at a casual family entertainment center.
- o Volunteer together if you have a common passion in a nonprofit.

---

[10] Catfished is having a relationship with someone on social media or dating apps that isn't who they say they are. Generally, they use someone else's photos and do not live where they say or live the lifestyle they say they have. The profile they present is dishonest and full of lies.

- Go on a group hike or group bike ride — after a few conversations!

Sex - I guess I have to go there.

- Chemistry is an amazing thing. When you are first 'on the market' and that first person comes along, allow yourself to feel through that. Remember in Chapter 2 with Faith? She said she healed so much with her first real sexual partner. She reclaimed her sexuality and her power. It can be life-changing.
- Sexually transmitted diseases are still around and mid-life age groups have a rise in cases because of casual sex and a lack of protection. Take precautions.
- There is a myth about third dates. Some people would have you believe that after a third date, sex is expected. It's up to you to establish the ground rules. My good friend has a three-month rule — wow, take that to the bank.
- Sexuality is important so don't play it down. But value yourself and your heart over chemistry. But if you are feeling it AND you feel safe, have fun!
- Having sex can be casual, but not everyone is comfortable with casual. If your emotions are tied to sex, then be completely honest with yourself about that. Honor this. It is very common to prefer that a trust and bond are formed before sex, so know and follow your heart.
- Bad sex also exists and it is not fun. If you have the patience to work through it, good for you. But if you value sexual chemistry in a relationship, don't fool yourself into thinking that a lack of chemistry might change. It is okay to highly value chemistry. A person can be both very kind and not

right for you.

I'm sure some of these have just instigated more questions for you. Hopefully this will spark conversations with you and your friends, your siblings or even your children.

Empowerment Practice 12: Make Your Profile

You have been doing a lot of hard things while going through this book. I've done these exercises multiple times with friends, coaches, teachers and therapists. They are hard things and hopefully you are getting good at doing the hard things.

Below are prompts that appear in dating apps. I want you to think through what you have learned and put it to use for yourself. NOTE: I'm not encouraging you to go get on an app.

I want you to see YOU through another's eyes.

What can you show the world about how special you are, what you have to offer and what brings you joy?

Have fun with this and if you use your answers on a profile, I wish you the best. Go have fun!

1. About me in 100 words or less.

2. My interests are:

3. Choose which of these is what you want: Relationship, Casual, Marriage, Not sure yet

4. To me, a happy relationship looks like:

5. My friends say I am:

6. The world is a great place because:

7. I hope you like to:

8. Never have I ever:

9. My ideal date is:

10. This year I really want to:

11. You can make me laugh by:

12. I get along best with people who:

13. My <u>love languages</u> are:

14. I love to relax by:

15. My greatest strength is:

EPILOGUE

Before you go…thank you for reading this book.

I believe all this information was shared with me so that I could share it with you. This wisdom has simply moved through me to you from a place of love and kindness.

Back in the preface, I mention that this book is like a moon simply reflecting the lessons. My friends' love and empathy is the sun, the light. Consider their gifts, absorb their light and go shine your light into the world.

The references at the end of the book are there in hopes that you will keep going. Let this book be a catalyst for your curiosity for life.

Become insatiable in your search of how to feel better, do better and live better.

My hope for you is that you recognize you are worthy of love, happiness and joy.

And that you are enough. You are so enough.

Yes, you are, and if you aren't sure about this — trust me that you will get there if you keep moving through it.

You have the power to get unstuck.

I had to trust others at one point to convince me that this was true.

I'm grateful they were there. I'm grateful to share with you.

REFERENCES

Camino de Santiago

Thomas, Katherine Woodward; *Calling in "The One"*

Brown, Brené; *The Call to Courage,* Netflix

West, Brianna; The Mind Journal website

Gray Ph.D.; John; *Men are from Mars, Women are from Venus*

Singer, Michael; *The Untethered Soul: The Journey Beyond Yourself*

Vanzant, Iyanla; *In the Meantime*

Byrne, Rhonda; *The Secret*

Byrne, Rhonda; *The Power*

Hill, Napoleon; *Outwitting the Devil*

Hill, Napoleon, *Think and Grow Rich*

Shinn, Florence; *The Complete Works of Florence Shin*

Wattles, Wallace D.' *The Science of Getting Rich*

Brown, Brené; *Daring Greatly: How the Courage to Be Vulnerable Transforms the Way We Live, Love, Parent, and Lead*

Berkowitz, Mildred Newman Bernard; *How To Be Your Own Best Friend*

Coehlo, Paulo; *The Pilgrimage*

Kubler-Ross, Elizabeth and Kessler, David; *On Grief and Grieving*

Tutu, Desmond, Dalai Lama, Abrams, Douglas; _The Book of Joy: Lasting Happiness in a Changing World_

Kahoot! Trivia app

Watkins, Steve; _Pilgrim Strong: Rewriting My Story on the Way of St. James_

Estevez, Emilio; _The Way_ movie

Young, Sarah; _Jesus Calling_

Sound Machine app on Apple

Sound Machine on Google Play

Lawson, Kara; _Handle Hard Stuff Better_ speech on Facebook

Chapman, Dr. Gary; _The Five Love Languages: The Secret to Love That Lasts_

ABOUT THE AUTHOR

C.K. Collins, aka Kelly, writes about her empowering five-year journey back to joy, happiness and love. Her inner healing has been a grassroots effort, surrounded by supportive friends and family, who held her hand, shared her pain and hugged her through a lot of tough moments following a traumatic divorce.

In gratitude and recognition of the gifts of love she has received, Kelly unfolds her ongoing journey to wholeness through storytelling and shares the lessons she learned from her friends all over the world.

Kelly owned her own company in the news publishing business and after she sold it, she took a two-year sabbatical. She is diving into writing books that empower people walking the tough path of loss. She believes that gratitude, empathy and love are the recipe for a fruitful and joyful life.

She originally hails from Tennessee and currently lives in the Northeast US. She has been traveling the world as often as possible. Her next books will include stories and lessons from her adventures and the amazing shifts in perspective acquired through solo travel.

With her beloved daughters is where she feels most wholly loved and seen.

Ingram Content Group UK Ltd.
Milton Keynes UK
UKHW021049300323
419409UK00005B/355